A Christian Response to COVID-19

EDITED BY
WALTER KASPER and
GEORGE AUGUSTIN

FOREWORD BY
POPE FRANCIS

Paulist Press
New York / Mahwah, NJ

Cover and book design by Lynn Else

First published in German as *Christsein in der Corona-Krise: Das Leben bezeugen in einer sterblichen Welt* by Matthias Grünewald Verlag, copyright © 2020. English-language edition published by Paulist Press, Inc., by permission of the Kardinal Walter Kasper Institut.

Library of Congress Control Number: 2020946845

ISBN 978-0-8091-5559-0 (paperback)
ISBN 978-1-58768-957-4 (e-book)

Published by Paulist Press
997 Macarthur Boulevard
Mahwah, New Jersey 07430
www.paulistpress.com

Printed and bound in the
United States of America

CONTENTS

FOREWORD

The corona crisis came over us like a sudden storm and profoundly changed our private, family, professional, and public lives. Many mourn the passing of dear relatives and friends. Many more have encountered economic trouble or have even lost their jobs. In many countries it became impossible to publicly celebrate the Eucharist at Easter, the highest feast of Christendom, and to receive strength and consolation through the sacraments.

This dramatic situation showed us human frailty and transience and our need for redemption. It shook many certainties on which we had based our existence, plans, and projects. The pandemic poses fundamental questions regarding our happiness in life and the treasure of our Christian faith.

The crisis is an alarm that lets us reflect on the deeper roots that anchor us during the storm. It reminds us that we have forgotten and neglected some important things in life and leads us to ponder what is really important and necessary, and what is only superficially important. It is a time of trial and of deciding to reconcile our lives more fully with God as our foundation and goal; it shows that in times of hardship we need solidarity with other people; it guides us to put ourselves at the service of others. It must shake us awake to worldwide injustice and awaken us to the cries of the poor and of our sick planet.

We celebrated Easter in the middle of the crisis and heard its message of life's victory over death. That message tells us that we Christians must not be paralyzed by the pandemic. Easter grants us hope, optimism, and courage, and strengthens us in our solidarity; it tells us to overcome past rivalries and to recognize ourselves across borders as part of one family in which each one carries the other's weight. The danger of infection by a virus is meant to teach us about a different type of "infection," an infection with love, which is transmitted from heart to heart. I am grateful for the many instances of spontaneous help and for the heroic sacrifices made by nurses, doctors, and priests. In these weeks we have felt the power of faith.

The initial phase of the corona crisis, in which there could be no public celebration of the Eucharist, was for many Christians a time of a painful, eucharistic fast. Many experienced the presence of the Lord where two or three congregated in his name. Televised transmission of the eucharistic feast was a makeshift solution that many were grateful for. But virtual transmission cannot replace the Lord's real presence. So I will be glad when we are able to return to normal, liturgical life. The presence of the resurrected Lord in his word and during the celebration of the Eucharist is meant to give us the power we need to tackle the difficult challenges that will follow the corona crisis.

I wish and hope that the theological considerations in this small book, *A Christian Response to COVID-19*, will bring about reflection and, for many, new hope and solidarity. As he was with the two disciples on the road to Emmaus, the Lord will also be with us in the future through his word and the breaking of the eucharistic bread. He will tell us, "Have no fear! I have conquered death."

Franciscus

PREFACE

The COVID-19 crisis surprised us like a sudden storm and all of a sudden changed the world and our personal lives. It has destroyed many livelihoods, incapacitated public life, including public church life, and nobody may tell how, and for how long, this crisis will persist. It is only certain that things will never be again as they were.

This booklet confronts the unique worldwide situation. It cannot and will not address all the many and manifold questions. Who could? It limits itself to existential questions concerning us as humans, as Christians, and as members of the Church. Each author writes from the personal experience he has lived through during the past weeks and months, from his Christian perspective, and from the matters within his personal responsibility. As expected, each of us has a different focus. However, all contributions have in common that they distance themselves from senseless extremist theories or even a postcrisis utopia, where one could seemingly reinvent both the Church and what it means to be Christian.

All contributions see meaning in the crisis in the way Pope Francis expressed in his foreword. The crisis has yet again made us aware of our transience, frailty, and mortality. It is an alarm signal that calls for rethinking, repentance, and renewal. It invites us to derive new hope, courage, energy, and happiness from the sources of life and faith, and to stand by those to whom the crisis has brought hardship and difficulty.

On behalf of myself and Fr. George Augustin, I wish to thank all authors for contributing on such short notice. I also thank the Patmos Publishing Group and the Matthias Grünewald Verlag for having brought this booklet out as soon as possible under the restraining conditions of the crisis. Dr. Ulrich Sander did the reader's work from home, applying his usual thoroughness. Pope Francis was the fastest of them all, as he reacted within three days to the request for a foreword. My gratitude goes to him especially.

Cardinal Walter Kasper

CHAPTER 1

COVID-19 AS DISRUPTION, UPHEAVAL, AND NEW BEGINNINGS

WALTER KASPER

HOW HAVE WE EXPERIENCED THE CRISIS?

For months now we have been in the grip of the COVID-19 crisis. Although all of us have been and are affected, we have experienced this crisis in very different ways: some of us being directly affected by the virus, others as relatives of the sick, caregivers, doctors, or pastoral workers. All of us are different. Often we have felt on edge in our family and professional lives, whether we are young or in high-risk groups, including the sick, the elderly, and the disabled, or those living in close proximity to others in prison or emergency shelters. And all our experiences have been different, according to whether we live in China, Italy, or even

Germany. The experience of regular churchgoers has also differed from that of nonchurchgoers or those who only sporadically attend church. The list could easily go on to include many moving individual stories.

So many individual experiences, and yet this is also one experience common to all of us, welding us to a shared destiny. We are all too used to hearing daily news reports of disasters. Yet they often occur in far-off places, in Asia or Africa. Now we are dealing with a genuine pandemic, literally meaning a crisis affecting all (*pân*) the people (*dêmos*), that is, all of us, both collectively and as individuals. For all of us, the pandemic has meant an abrupt hiatus from our previous lifestyle, from the everyday habits and assumptions we took for granted. It is affecting not only our individual lives, but the whole of public life, bringing the world to an unprecedented standstill. Once bustling cities, busy airports, and sport and entertainment centers have turned into deserts overnight, and no one can say with any certainty how long all this will last.

What is happening does not only affect the external aspects of private and public life, it reaches the very heart of the modern world. Basic human rights, including the freedom of movement, personal contact, and freedom of assembly, have been restricted to the absolute minimum, while last but certainly not least, the exercise of collective public worship has also been prohibited. Until now, such phenomena have only occurred in totalitarian states, but today this is happening in liberal states where most citizens are complying with this extraordinary situation, which—barring a few complaints—they accept as reasonable.

I can still remember the last years and months of the Second World War. Very often we did not know how or where we would wake up the following morning, or even if we would wake up at all. But life didn't come to a complete standstill: it went on, albeit often amid considerable challenges. Many churches had been destroyed, but liturgical celebrations were still held in those that were open. Now, in contrast, even during Easter, the most important feast of Christianity, no public communal act of worship was held in Rome. This was quite unprecedented in nearly two thousand years of the history of the Church.

Nothing highlighted this situation, unique in world history, quite so much as the pope's *urbi et orbi* blessing uttered before the medieval plague crucifix from the church of San Marcello al Corso in Rome. In 1522, the year of the plague, a great, crowded procession followed this crucifix through Rome. Now the pope was alone before this crucifix, facing an almost ghostly St. Peter's Square, speaking as though into the void, although via media he was being followed across the world. There was no liturgical celebration of Easter, the greatest feast for the Christians of the East and of the West, no celebration of Pesach for the Jews, which they have celebrated for over two thousand years. Neither did the Muslims mark Ramadan, the month of fasting, with communal prayers in mosques that conclude with a feast to break the fast. None of this had ever happened before.

The origins of the virus are still not completely clear. Was it due to human carelessness, a laboratory accident, or is this more like a natural disaster, akin to an earthquake, an erupting volcano, a tornado, or a tsunami? We all knew and understood such devastating natural disasters were possible at any time in certain areas, just like the epidemics that, year after year, claim many thousands of victims. But this virus, which has spread rapidly across the world, was quite unknown until now, and our highly developed medical science has not yet found a cure. It demonstrates in a new way altogether the vulnerability and fragility of human beings, our limitations, and our impotence in the face of the forces of nature. It casts into question anew our faith in progress and feasibility. This is an entirely new, unique, and extreme experience of contingency.

To be fair, we should add that during this contingency there have been many positives. Most people have responded with a great deal of common sense, with often-surprising creativity and frequently with admirable solidarity. Countless reports are circulating about the extreme selflessness of health workers, doctors, and pastors, about the young people volunteering to help the elderly, and neighbors helping each other. Meanwhile, families have reorganized living arrangements in the confined spaces of their homes, with all the consequent strain this implies. Outside the narrow circle of their own family, people live at a greater physical distance from each other than before, yet are far more aware than previously how much they share bonds of solidarity, bound together by a common destiny.

As was only realistically to be expected, there have also been and continue to be examples of ruthless and ingenious criminal exploitation of the crisis. But the astonishing thing is what has emerged overall: the human capacity for drawing on inner resources, to rise above our own interests. This gives the lie to negative, judgmental generalizations about the world and youth of today. This revelation, that people possess far more internal resources than might seem superficially to be the case, gives rise to the hope that we so urgently need now.

Thus, even though we harbor reasonable hope of finding a vaccine at some point, life after the crisis will not be the same as before. Already, we need to ask ourselves, how will we deal with the post-COVID crisis?

You don't need to be an ingrained pessimist to believe the forecasts of grave long-term economic and therefore social and political repercussions. We will all be poorer, to a greater or lesser degree, and this will spark social disorder, political conflicts, and in Europe above all, a restructuring of the international order.

The consequences of COVID-19 are comparable to those of the devastating Lisbon earthquake of 1755. More than 250 years later, we still do not know exactly what caused this natural catastrophe. What we do know is that this devastating earthquake shook contemporary culture to the core, transforming both culture and the philosophy of the Enlightenment. The earthquake signified an end to optimism and faith in the progress of the Enlightenment. A whole era in European history ended.

The COVID-19 crisis will also rattle our assumptions as a civilization, as a society, and as cultures: these are consequences that today almost no one can anticipate in detail. Through medicine, we will beat COVID-19, but on an intellectual, cultural, and also theological level, the virus will retain its hold over us for some time to come.

HOW CAN WE UNDERSTAND THE CRISIS?

The theological question surrounding the Lisbon earthquake was one of theodicy: How could a good and all-powerful God allow such a disaster? In the nineteenth century, this issue was considered the "rock of atheism" (Georg Büchner). In the twentieth century, the issue of theodicy gained new relevance in the wake of the unspeakable crimes associated with the name Auschwitz. With the terrible murder of millions of people, chillingly planned and coldly executed on an industrial scale, Western European culture, as we knew it, went up in smoke with the fumes from the gas chambers of Auschwitz.

The COVID-19 crisis is a different beast. Even at the beginning, when there may have been human error, this was not a man-made crisis but rather a natural disaster of global dimensions. It is what philosophy terms a contingent event, that is, an event that is not inevitable because of a natural law but that is nevertheless perfectly possible. It does not need to happen, but there is obviously a possibility that it might, and it is something that happens to us and affects us (*contingere*).[1]

As it is a problem of contingency, we need to speak of COVID-19 in philosophical and theological terms. The question is, How can human beings cope with this and many other types of inevitable contingency in life and reality? This is not an abstract question, but rather an existential and very definite one, whose reach—as I hope to show—has a widespread impact on political and ecclesial questions.

It is not a new problem. The Greeks were fascinated by the order and beauty of the cosmos. Today, we know much more about the remarkable order that prevails in the macro as much as in the microcosm, even at the level of atoms and subatomic particles and the tiniest living cellular and genetic structures. But Aristotle already knew of the problem of contingency, while today, we know from quantum theory and the theory of relativity (Werner Heisenberg and Albert Einstein), not to mention chaos theory, that reality does not operate, as Isaac Newton thought in the seventeenth and eighteenth centuries, like a large mechanical clock. Or that the evolution of the universe after the initial Big Bang and from the amoebas until *Homo sapiens* did not happen in a linear fashion, but instead needs to be understood according to the law of chance and necessity (Jacques Monod).

Following Aristotle, Thomas Aquinas explored the problem of contingency further. He poses the problem in principle, in the context of the whole of reality, as a fundamental question of metaphysics. This would later be formulated by Leibniz, Schelling, and Heidegger as follows: "Why is there something rather than nothing?" Everything that is real is evidently possible, but not necessary: it could be something else, or it could not be at all. So why is it not nothing? Why is it something? This is only possible, according to Thomas, if there is something that cannot fail to exist, that is, something that is necessary. This is what everyone calls God.[2] This is what is described as the third of Aquinas's five proofs of the existence of God. But Thomas himself was sage enough not to refer to five proofs, but rather five ways toward God, that is, five ways to show that faith in God, which at the time was universally taken for granted, was intellectually justifiable and therefore consistent with reason.

God is the ultimate cause of all created beings: he is present in all that is and all that happens, but at the same time is above all things. By giving being to all that exists and allowing it to be, he desires it to have its own autonomy, existence, behavior, and laws.[3] That is why it is impossible to immediately attribute a natural disaster to

God or to declare or warn that it is a divine punishment. Nor should we interpret success and prosperity as a divine reward for good behavior, or as a sign of God's special election as claimed by the *prosperity theology* preached in some churches.[4] The misery of pseudotheological justification is revealed in the Old Testament Book of Job. However much everything that is and that happens may be ultimately founded on divine providence, the thoughts of God are not our thoughts: as high as heaven is above the earth, so God's thoughts are above our thoughts (see Isa 55:8–9).[5]

To make room for faith, Kant also subjected the proofs of God, and with them the entire metaphysical edifice, to a fundamental critique from which the proofs of God have not entirely recovered. Whatever judgment Kant's critique may merit, he made it clear that the proofs of God's existence depend on many ontological and epistemological presuppositions that may be justified, but that many people will also dispute. Their weakness lies in the fact that people cannot be compelled by the force of deductive logic to assent to proofs of something as important as the existence of God. This must be a free act of will.

This is the standpoint from which Kant tackled the issue anew. He started with the freedom of human beings and made it clear that our freedom can only be meaningful if the world we live in offers room for freedom. This, in turn, is only possible if human freedom and nature are determined and encompassed by a greater freedom. God is, therefore, a hypothesis of freedom. Following Kant, this led Fichte, Schelling, and Hegel to the great systematic schema of Idealism, which, from a starting point of an absolute freedom, understands the world and history as one great history of freedom.

If we assert that everything is reasonable, the question arises, Where do the many unreasonable things that exist in the world come from, especially the destructive force of evil, so present throughout the history of humanity? Under the relentless onslaught of contingency events, Idealism-based systems have collapsed. The contingent world will not fit smoothly into one system.[6] Marx sought to turn the Hegelian system upside-down and interpret Hegel's ideas as a reflection of socioeconomic conditions. Friedrich Nietzsche sought to understand God as an expression of resentment. For him the death of God was the good news that heralded the age of the superman.[7] Ultimately, postmodern thought has declared all metanarratives to be dead, Idealism as well as Marxism.[8]

By deconstructing God, the postidealist and postmodern age faces a genuine problem. Human beings now find themselves alone and lost in a wide and not always friendly world. As the mature Schelling—and later Kierkegaard and Heidegger—concluded, humankind is consequently overcome by fear. This is the basic condition of modern man and woman. If God is no longer useful, if he is no longer needed or has become indifferent toward us, then we human beings must take hold of the problem of contingency, adopting the role of providence ourselves.

That is just what modern bourgeois society has done. It tries to dominate nature, or at the very least protect itself from nature's wickedness. Contemplative reasoning has become an exercise in technological-instrumental reasoning that depends on whatever is feasible. Nature becomes mere matter and as such, is exploited. Added to this is the provision of general interest—the economy. No longer is the economy merely a necessary means for providing services of general interest. It has turned into the very content, meaning, and purpose of our existence. What counts is achievement and success. Objects are valued for their usefulness and exchange value, and above all, for their monetary value. For this to work, society must be properly managed and organized. It requires a bureaucratic form of governance that controls and regulates everything democratically as far as possible. Politics is thus reduced to an exercise in planning, dictated by objective constraints. The supreme goal is security.

It did not take COVID-19 to show that this story doesn't add up. Our repeated financial crises have already made it clear that unbridled capitalism divides society and nations into the rich and poor and kills people. The ecological crisis has led us to see that our irreverent approach to and unscrupulous exploitation of nature make the earth uninhabitable and destroy the very basis of life itself. The COVID-19 crisis has led to a virtual shutdown of the economy and brought our society to a standstill. This ultimately strikes at the heart of the liberal bourgeois political order. The virus has challenged the bourgeois sense of security. Contingency has caught us out.

Bourgeois society has also realized that complete security is impossible: there will always be an element of risk. Neither life, nor to a far greater degree, death, are really within our grasp. That is why religion is indispensable. We need it in order to cope with contingency: now its role is to console us.[9] Through faith we know that the world is neither fatalistic nor deterministic, yet neither is it left to pure chance. We may trust in the providence of God and know that we are, deep down, sustained by him.[10]

However, this kind of bourgeois liberal religion only offers one bleak consolation. For in this context, religion and faith lack intrinsic value, as they have been appropriated and are only functional. Faith transcends without transcendence (Ernst Bloch), in a symbolic elevation of something that, in any case, already exists. The contextual conditions do not change at all but on the contrary are stabilized. Thus, civil religion is an ideology of the bourgeois worldview. As a cultural ingredient, it continues to be respected and appreciated, because technology and the economy alone cannot satisfy the needs of the soul, the need for ethical instruction or for aesthetics. Like everything else, religion is a consumer product that exists to satisfy a need. And the Church turns into a provider of services.

From the start, Søren Kierkegaard offered a critique of bourgeois Christianity that had wide-reaching repercussions. According to Kierkegaard, Christians have stifled Christianity by eliminating the scandal of the Christian message.[11] Christianity survives in a state of sluggish complacency, utterly lacking in passion.[12] It has become a triumphant Church whose interiority is hidden and that no longer appears to be the Church militant.[13]

Two martyrs of the twentieth century followed in Kierkegaard's footsteps. In his *Letters and Papers from Prison*, Dietrich Bonhoeffer criticizes how God is evicted from the world as soon as it comes of age and is only useful as a stopgap for answering the so-called ultimate big questions.[14] Alfred Delp recognized the former greatness of the bourgeois way of life, now buried beneath every conceivable kind of security and insurance policy, producing the kind of person "to whose heart one might almost say God himself could find no access." This kind of bourgeois person has also become typical of the Church through its possessions, power, careful existence, and secure lifestyle. The bureaucratic Church is, in large part, the work of bourgeois humanity.[15]

In the field of theology, it was above all the figure of Johann Baptist Metz, who, following on from Max Horkheimer and Theodor Adorno, revealed the internal dialectic of the Enlightenment,[16] and criticized transcendental and existential theology for introducing a bourgeoise mentality into theology and the Church. Both have succumbed to the embrace of the Enlightenment.[17] Neither theology nor the Church can overcome their state of crisis because they use the power of Beelzebub to expel the devil and are selling themselves to bourgeois mores.

Thus, Christianity finds itself like a tree stripped of leaves after an autumn storm. Are the empty churches, the empty St. Peter's Square, therefore, an outer symbol of an inner emptiness? Are the empty churches, as Nietzsche sneered, the mausoleum of a dead God? No! For Peter stood there in the form of his successor, announcing the Resurrection: *Christus vivit*. He has resurrected from the dead. On this foundation the Church must think again. On this rock of the gospel it may build.

HOW CAN THE CHURCH OVERCOME THE CRISIS?

It is neither the duty nor the responsibility of the Church and theology to suggest an exit strategy for the COVID crisis, nor to resolve its subsequent financial, social, and political challenges. What can be expected of the Church is some basic guidance, which in the context of these pages, may only be sketched out in a few brief paragraphs.[18]

1. As Christians, we first need to know who we are, what we live by, and what we hope for. For me, it was no mere coincidence that the crisis became particularly apparent over Easter. At Easter the stone that covers the tomb is taken away, bringing the good news that God gives life to the dead.[19] It doesn't fit into any preexisting framework. Easter testifies to the sovereign freedom of God. This is acutely counterfactual. Refusing any kind of accommodation with preexisting ideas, Easter opens new horizons. It is pure contingency but at the same time a testimony of the unwavering fidelity of God through which we gain firm ground on which to stand in the face of the world's inconsistency. We can only refer to the kingdom of God with images and parables, but the saying "the kingdom of God and his justice" shows that this message is far from indifferent to the flagrant injustice of the contemporary world. It is about more than simply satisfying needs, or a future planned by technocrats and controlled by computers. This is no otherworldly utopia or shout of hurrah, rather an amen,[20] a quiet, "yes, that is how it is." And thus, it is a call to turn away from false idols, and at the same time, a mission, sending us forth into the world.

2. The new creation begun at Easter refers us back to the first creation. Already in Genesis, humanity receives the global commission to protect and

care for the earth. This commission is immediately developed and elevated through the founding of the Sabbath, which interrupts the working and economic order by establishing the rhythm of time. The sanctification of the Sabbath affirms that the human being is not just a creature made for labor and that Sabbath rest does not mean resting from work to recharge one's batteries in order to work more. It means resting to have time for God and for people, for one's family, one's friends, and social interaction in general. The time of God is the time of humanity. And the glory of God is humanity fully alive (St. Irenaeus of Lyons). Worship and entertainment, worship and culture are now interconnected. To a world that has no time, only knowing rest and rushing, we need to say, this is the time to have time. To survive in a way that is truly human, we require a new Sabbath order.

3. The new creation does not begin on Easter morning, but had already begun on Holy Saturday. The *descensus ad inferos* is little valued in the Western Church, but in the Eastern Churches, it is at the heart of Easter.[21] Jesus descends to the shadowy kingdom of death and the dead. This is the victory over power itself and the powers of death. It is solidarity with the dead, the murdered, the forgotten, with all those who lack a future and live in the shadow of death, because they are regarded as of little value and therefore cast aside. This is something more than a silent memory of the dead and a culture of remembrance: it is a reminder for the here and now that

we are raised up on the shoulders of those who have preceded us. Their names are permanently inscribed in the memory of God, through whom they now live and rest in peace. Without this origin we have no future. This runs counter to a unilateral direction pointing only toward progress and the future, which, lacking any sense of its origin, has lost its way.

4. Easter is the feast of Christian freedom. *Freedom* is a big word, the key word of modernity. We cannot give it up: we must defend it. But Christian freedom has nothing to do with a cold, calculating, selfish freedom, or the cult of self-fulfillment that instantly turns into self-pity, neither does it have anything at all to do with random personal choices. This is a liberated, redeemed freedom made effective through love (see Gal 5:1, 6). It is free of attachment to the self, and because of this, it is free to be there for others. It is shown through sharing, through solidarity, where one person bears another's burdens (see Gal 6:2). Mercy takes care of particular contingent needs. Necessity is not to be seen as purely defined by welfare cases catered to through the social welfare system. It is justice related to individual cases of real penury. Through his wounds the disciples recognized the risen Lord. The identity card of the Christian is to see Jesus Christ through the wounds of the Body of Christ—the Church—present in a hidden way throughout the history of humanity since the time of Abel the just (Matt 25).[22] The Church must be present in the world as a gift for others:

it is only a Church if it is a Church for others.[23] Its future lies in a return to *diakonia*.[24] This is the Church acting as an emergency field hospital (Pope Francis).

5. The resurrected Christ appeared to the disciples during meals. Easter and the Eucharist are inseparably linked to each other. The worst thing about Easter this year was the absence of public celebrations of the Eucharist. Worse still, according to some surveys, only a relative minority actually noticed. The pope gave a countersign in St. Peter's Square: his unusual *urbi et orbi* blessing. He imparted this with the monstrance, thus showing us that we will only have a life and a future with the eucharistic bread of life. The Eucharist is a meal and we cannot share the bread of the Eucharist without also sharing our daily bread. Paul teaches us that we should not separate the two tables, although we should distinguish between them (see 1 Cor 11:34). Therefore, the Eucharist is not only a meal. That is why adoration of the blessed sacrament preceded the blessing with the monstrance in St. Peter's Square. Jesus himself celebrated the Last Supper in the light of the eschatological meal in the kingdom of God. That brings us to Revelation, the last book of the Bible, in which the celebration of the Eucharist is described as an echo and anticipation of the heavenly liturgy before the immolated and glorified Lamb, whose blood has made us kings and priests (see 5:8–10). To grasp this, we have a long road ahead of us in the Paschal renovation of the liturgy.

6. The oldest Easter testimony of the New Testament has already revealed that there is no Easter testimony without Easter witnesses, above all Peter and the Twelve (see 1 Cor 15:3–5). Certainly, every Christian receives the light of Easter in baptism and should bear witness to this. But there were genuine witnesses: the apostles. The night before his death, Jesus showed them how to conduct their essential ministry through the clear example he gave them by washing their feet. Thus, he turned the social hierarchy on its head, pointing downward: the apostles were not to dominate but to serve others as slaves. In fact, all the apostles he called died as martyrs. This is something to bear in mind when we speak of the future way of life of priests (and bishops).[25]

We have had an example of this: St. Martin of Tours, patron of my home church and diocese. By dividing his cloak in half, he became, and remains today, a symbol of Christian charity. A mosaic in San Vitale in Ravenna also depicts him as first in the line of confessors who were disciples of St. Hilary, the father of the Church who defended the true divinity of Jesus Christ against the Arians. Finally, according to his biographer, Sulpicius Severus, Martin retained the monastic pre-Constantinian ideal of the bishop after Constantine's change of heart on Christianity. This was at a time when most bishops adapted with surprising speed to the imperial Church. For me, St. Martin is a bishop for all ages, the model of a bishop in the episcopal nonclerical Church of the post-Constantine era: he is rightly the patron of a Church in renewal following COVID-19.

Notes

1. See "Kontingenz," *Historisches Wörterbuch der Philosophie* 4 (Darmstadt: Wissenschaftl. Buchges., 1976), 1027–38.

2. Aquinas, *Summa theologica* I q. 1 a. 3; *Summa contra gentiles* I, 13.

3. *Summa theologica* I q. 8 a.1–3. The Second Vatican Council has explicitly taught that all reality, whether created or cultural, enjoys relative autonomy, see *Gaudium et spes* 36, etc.

4. The theory posited by Max Weber in *Die protestantische Ethik und der Geist des Kapitalismus* (Tübingen: Mohr, 1904; Eng. trans.: *The Protestant Ethic and the Spirit of Capitalism* [n.p.: Andesite Press, 2015]) according to which the Reformed Protestant mind understands success and well-being as a reward for sacrifice and self-denial. This theory established the basis and legitimacy of capitalist thought.

5. Stephan Weber, *Warum greift der gute Gott nicht ein? Die Allmacht Gottes in zeitgenössischen theologischen Ansätzen und das Problem des* malum naturale (Freiburg i. Br.: Herder, 2013).

6. This is not to say that vulgarized Idealism does not lack small yet fallacious convictions. The saying, "If the facts don't fit my formulations, to hell with the facts," is attributed to Hegel. Likewise, it is said that Albert Einstein replied to a question about a possible proof of reality that countered his theory with the words, "Then, I would feel sorry for the good Lord. The theory is correct." Christian Morgenstern, putting this in his own words, quipped, "For, he reasons pointedly, that which must not, cannot be." Today, a postfact world has emerged: when

the facts don't fit our preconceived opinions, they must be cast aside. One therefore finds alternative facts, which constitute fake news, but which if they fit with our preexisting prejudice, lend it strength and a semblance of good faith.

7. F. Nietzsche, *Die fröhliche Wissenschaft*, ed. Karl Schlechta (Munich: Hanser, 1963), 126ff.; Eng. trans.: *The Gay Science* (New York: Random House, 1974).

8. Jean-François Lyotard, *Das postmoderne Wissen*, ed. Peter Engelmann (Vienna: Passagen, 2012); Eng. trans.: *The Postmodern Condition: A Report on Knowledge* (Minneapolis: University of Minnesota Press, 2010).

9. H. Lübbe, *Religion nach der Aufklärung* (Graz: Styria, 1986).

10. See Hans Küng, *Christsein* (München, 1974); Eng. trans.: *On Being a Christian* (New York: Continuum, 2008). It is no accident this book has become a bestseller, but it needs defending from precipitate judgment as the author, because he originally followed the theology of Karl Barth, is inoculated against a major relapse into liberal theology.

11. Søren Kierkegaard, *Einübung ins Christentum* (1850), Gesammelte Werke Bd. 26 (Düsseldorf: Eugen Diederichs Verlag), 101–5; Eng. trans.: *Practice in Christianity* (Princeton, NJ: Princeton University Press, 1991).

12. Kierkegaard, *Einübung ins Christentum*, 115.

13. Kierkegaard, *Einübung ins Christentum*, 210–11; 218ff.

14. Dietrich Bonhoeffer, *Widerstand und Ergebung. Briefe und Aufzeichnungen aus der Haft*, ed. Eberhard Bethge (Munich: Siebenstern Taschenbuch Verlag, 1977), 356–57, 373ff.; Eng. trans.: *Letters and Papers from Prison* (London: SCM Press, 2017).

15. Alfred Delp, *Im Angesicht des Todes* (Frankfurt a. M.: Carolusdruckerei, 1961), 210–13; Eng. trans.: *The Prison Meditations of Father Alfred Delp*, intro. Thomas Merton (New York: Herder and Herder, 1963).

16. Max Horkheimer and Theodor W. Adorno, *Dialektik der Aufklärung* (Frankfurt a. M.: Fischer, 1969); Eng. trans.: *Dialectic of Enlightenment* (Stanford, CA: Stanford University Press, 2002).

17. Johann Baptist Metz, *Glaube in Geschichte und Gesellschaft: Studien zu einer praktischen Fundamentaltheologie* (Mainz: Herder, 1977); Eng. trans.: *Faith in History and Society: Toward a Practical, Fundamental Theology* (New York: Crossroad, 2007). And from another perspective, Benedict XVI—as a representative example of his many publications, I refer in particular to Jurgen Habermas and Joseph Ratzinger, *Dialektik der Säkularisierung: Über Vernunft und Religion* (Bonn : Bundeszentrale für politische Bildung, 2005); Eng. trans.: *The Dialectics of Secularization* (San Francisco: Ignatius, 2006).

18. In my initial lecture in Münster, "Dogma and the Word of God" (1964), after examining Idealism in the mature Schelling, I posited the foundation of a mature gospel-based theology I have tried to develop ever since: WKGS 7, 2015; Eng. trans.: *Dogma and the Word of God: The Absolute in History*, The Collected Works of Walter Kasper (Mahwah, NJ: Paulist Press, 2018).

19. On this point, the declaration of the Synod of Wurzburg, *Our Hope* (1971–75) is worth a read.

20. Kierkegaard, *Einübung ins Christentum*, 110.

21. Hans Urs von Balthasar on the theology of Holy Saturday may be found in *Mysterium salutis* 3/2 (Einsideln, 1969); Eng. trans.: *And Still We Wait: Hans Urs*

Von Balthasar's Theology of Holy Saturday and Christian Discipleship, Princeton Theological Monographs (Eugene, OR: Pickwick Publications, 2018).

22. Vatican II, Dogmatic Constitution on the Church, *Lumen Gentium* 2.

23. Bonhoeffer, *Widerstand und Ergebung*, 413.

24. Delp, *Im Angesicht des Todes*, 139–40.

25. Some people may object that Mary Magdalene was the first Easter witness (John 20:11–18). Indeed, she is rightly venerated as *apostola apostolorum*. She gave the woebegone, resigned, and frightened apostles a good shake-up. This fits in perfectly with the concept developed by Edith Stein of the role and mission of women in the Church. Christ has called them into intimate union with him, "to be emissaries of his love, proclaimers of His will to kings and popes, and forerunners of His Kingdom in the hearts of men....[It] is the most sublime vocation which has been given, and whoever sees this way open before her will yearn for no other way." *Beruf des Mannes und der Frau nach der Natur- und Gnadenordnung*, WW 5 (Louvain-Freiburg, 1959), 43; Eng. trans.: "The Separate Vocations of Man and Woman according to Nature and Grace," in *Essays on Woman*, 2nd ed., The Collected Works of Edith Stein (Washington, DC: ICS Publications, 1996).

CHAPTER 2

BEARING WITNESS TO LIFE IN A WORLD OF DEATH

George Augustin, SAC

Bearing witness to life in a world of death: that is the subtitle of the German version of the book in which this chapter was originally published. We want to reflect on the life to which as Christians we must bear witness. In a world of death, the Christian faith proclaims eternal life to be the hope that allows humanity to live and die. It is up to us to draw strength from that hope so we can shape with wisdom both our lives and the world around us.

THE COVID-19 CRISIS AND ITS GLOBAL REPERCUSSIONS

In January 2020, the president of China, Xi Jinping, informed the world of the outbreak of the pandemic, explaining that this dangerous virus was spread through human contact. Since then, COVID-19, caused by the virus SARS-CoV-2, the trigger for the pandemic, has struck fear and terror across the world. COVID-19 has wreaked havoc in every part of the globe. Five months after the pandemic emerged, the situation is still extremely tense. Even though the numbers of those infected are now going down in many countries, the fight against the virus is still far from won. It will still be a long time before an effective vaccine and medicines are found and placed within the reach of all. A new outbreak of the virus is feared, and the world could once again be brought to a standstill. It is likely that we will have to live with COVID-19 and its attendant phenomena for some time. We must learn to live with it. It is also quite possible that once this virus is beaten, another will challenge us, confronting us once more with biological danger.

COVID-19 has brought a root-and-branch change to our lives. This crisis is unknown, a medical, financial, human, and spiritual challenge without precedent that will decisively shape the years to come. Although we cannot yet predict the full reach of the crisis, far less foresee when the pandemic will end, we do know that it will remain a fundamental challenge for humanity: not the pandemic itself but the existential anguish and insecurity brought about by the crisis. Many people have suddenly become aware of their own vulnerability and fragility, while many of our presumed sources of security have vanished into thin air as our planet's lifestyle is questioned to the core. Unexpectedly, all of us have been brought face-to-face with death and sickness, and life-threatening health risks. Being confronted by the limits of our own lives has overwhelmed us, and we are faced with a fear of the future previously unknown or buried deep within us.

Before our very eyes, we see the sudden collapse of the system that has dictated our modern lifestyle.

The COVID-19 crisis is a real imposition on humanity. We find ourselves facing a time of change with serious social and financial consequences, on top of an immense burden of interpersonal and psychological pressures. COVID-19 has caught the world unawares, like a thief in the night. When the disease was spreading through the Chinese city of Wuhan, little did the world imagine that it would become a pandemic. This development shows with inescapable clarity that our world is one community that, for good or ill, shares a common destiny.

The COVID-19 crisis has brought many people death, immense suffering and anxiety, and existential fear, as well as triggering a serious worldwide financial crisis of incalculable consequence to date. The virus has left the world in a state of shock. The pandemic seems, furthermore, to be degenerating into an "infodemic" of conspiracy theories, rumors, and misleading news reports that threaten to pollute our world: malign spirits are circulating and, intentionally or not, increasing people's fears. That is why it is crucial to adopt a perspective of prudence, common sense, and responsibility while we face the global repercussions of this crisis. Obviously, it is too early for any conclusive analysis of what is happening, or indeed to interpret the crisis or reach any kind of balanced evaluation.

This epidemic has spread across the globe, affecting directly or indirectly every single person on the planet, so it counts as a major crisis, one that the world has never experienced on this scale. That is why we are now at a decisive turning point in world history. Thus, the COVID-19 crisis offers a major opportunity to contemplate human life, in all its multifaceted glory, from the perspective of the Christian faith. In fact, every human being, regardless of their religious convictions, is called upon to reflect on this global crisis and discover for him or herself its existential meaning. The COVID-19 crisis is and continues to be a disaster of apocalyptic proportions that we must get through. So why is this crisis happening? This question is inadequate. Perhaps we should ask instead, what is the point of this crisis? It is down to each one of us to discover what we might learn from it and what each of us might do to ensure that our globally connected world recovers and is better than before the crisis.

In this context, some major questions arise: Does this crisis have any meaning? Can it help us to reflect anew on the perennial question of the meaning of human life? Might our present experiences make us freshly aware of any neglected or forgotten aspects of life? Do we appreciate the gift of life? Are we aware that our lifespan on earth is limited? How should we understand the mystery of death? What can we learn about life after death from this experience? Which boundaries should we accept and establish with the world around us? On what basis can we humanize our culture and construct a new sense of humanity? How much attention do we pay to people at risk, those who are sick, weak, alone, or needy in any way? Which core values do we need to rediscover? Should we rethink the habits we take for granted and change our lifestyle?

We can safely say that our world is not going to be the same as it was before the COVID-19 crisis. The question of what this terrible crisis does or does not mean is raised by its apocalyptic scale, the experience of human destitution, and our ensuing anxieties about the future. We are not yet in a place to give a fully satisfactory reply to all of this. All we can say so far amounts to guesswork and a tentative bid to understand or interpret the crisis.

What is beyond doubt is that this crisis implies a questioning of our faith. It is a time of doubt, of being on the edge of life, of faith put to the test. The COVID-19 crisis is a sign of the times, and we must seek answers to our questions and difficulties from the depth and fruitfulness of the Christian faith. This faith leads us to refocus on our personal relationship with God. Our priority can only lie in seeking personal answers to the crisis, and reframing our anxieties, stress, and consequently our attitudes, through a new, faith-filled perspective.

GOD, THE AUTHOR AND FINISHER OF OUR LIVES

The uncertainty triggered by the COVID-19 crisis offers an opportunity to change our perspective and widen our horizons. This change of perspective recognizes that God, not the human race, is at the center of everything. The Christian faith professes God to be the Creator of the visible and invisible world who sustains and perfects this world. It is time to rediscover God again as the Creator and custodian of life. He is the origin of life, bestowing life upon us. He alone can preserve or end life. We come from God, living in his presence in this world until our lives end, peaking with our return to him. Only in God does humanity find a satisfactory answer to the big questions of life. God is *the* answer to the human question about meaning. God, and not humanity, is the Lord of life. Faith in God gives the believer certainty and unshakeable hope: God has saved the world through his Son Jesus Christ, who through his death has overcome our own, and who gives us a share in eternal life, life in its fullness. The believer lives in the certainty that God will create a new life out of death.

The reality of God is unlike any other. He is "a God who hides himself" (Isa 45:15), who no one has ever seen (see John 1:18) and who "dwells in unapproachable light" (1 Tim 6:16), and because of this, we experience him as a very profound mystery. St. Augustine formulated the incomprehensibility of God with concision when he remarked that "if you have been able to comprehend it, you have comprehended something else instead of God."[1] This unfathomable, hidden character of God can be painfully clear in times of crisis. But walking through the darkness when he is hidden is part of our experience of God. It is reasonable for believers to hope that this unfathomable God should give us life and say yes to us. Humanity experiences God in an existential tension that swings between a joyful closeness and oppressive distance, between presence and absence, immanence and transcendence. The signs and seasons of God alternate like day and night, light and darkness, between feeling safe in God and feeling abandoned by him.

In the context of such experiences, we need to see again the treasures of our faith and renew our trust in God. We believe in a God who is the fullness of life and who frees us so that we might live. The God of life liberates us from all our addictions, bondages, and habits of self-alienation. Union with God allows humanity to recognize and develop true greatness. Through the light of God, the ultimate destiny of the world and of humankind is made manifest. A relationship with God brings the individual into a deeper relationship with others. As individuals, we are not isolated before God, but part of a community that supports us. Each of us receives an individual calling that at the same time connects us to many other people. Each of us has an irreplaceable and singular importance for others, and therefore for the community. This unique, unmistakable calling and community focus are not mutually exclusive but intrinsically interconnected. The community focus of each individual should be understood within a universal context. This is because a person, as part of a community, exists within the greater context of the whole of humanity and of creation.

The human being who is in relationship with the Creator knows that this relationship with God is the basic prerequisite for a balanced relationship with him- or herself, for living peacefully with others, and in harmony with creation. The person who admits God is their Creator knows that we cannot sustain creation without him. We need to be aware that nature is not everything and that hostile forces may exist in nature that place our lives in danger. That is why we must learn to see our world from God's perspective: there is a qualitative difference between seeking help from God and wanting to have everything under our control. The believer does everything humanly possible themself, while being well aware that only God can provide the final outcome:

> From where will my help come?
> My help comes from the LORD,
>   who made heaven and earth. (Ps 121:1–2)

The impotence of humanity reveals the strength of God, as "power is made perfect in weakness" (2 Cor 12:9).

Through human impotence, divine glory is made visible, even at times when this may not be immediately obvious to the believer.

From the Christian perspective, the mystery of human life in this world may be adequately interpreted only through God. Christianity understands the human person as a created being who is radically dependent on God. Human beings are totally receptive to God, both in their being and in their behavior. People are only completely themselves when they grow beyond themselves. Realizing this will lead to the awareness that our very being is God-given and we need to recognize our human limitations. Conversely, one who knows and acknowledges their limitations is aware that they depend on God: "For not by might can one prevail" (1 Sam 2:9). That is why it is a matter of existential significance to gaze at the one who can save us.

The COVID-19 crisis is challenging us to address our human condition and existence in the world in relation to God. The crisis lays bare everything that was not right beforehand in our lives and world. We still don't know how long this situation is going to last. But what we should realize is that after the crisis, we should not go back to the old sense of what was "normal." This crisis has made us painfully aware of many limitations in our lives at present, whether those separating us due to "social distancing," parting different generations within the same family, or others due to the closure, again, of national borders. These limitations make us distant from one another: often we only see others as potential carriers of the virus. In fact, this experience draws our attention to a deeper truth about human life: that it is limited and fragile.

The Psalmist has already told us that humanity must recognize its own limitations in order to grow in wisdom: "So teach us to count our days that we may gain a wise heart" (Ps 90:12). We can amplify this sentiment and say, Lord, teach us to recognize and accept our limitations. By doing so, we will gain wisdom of heart and learn how to structure our lives. This self-knowledge will help us to accept the *conditio humana*, the limitations of our existence. The need to recognize our limitations is already clear in the story of creation. Adam must recognize his limitations. His transgression means separation from intimacy with God, a distancing from him and a weakened relationship with him. Thus, this challenging time of pandemic can also become a time of grace in which we seek and experience God's consoling intimacy and find refuge in his protection.

UNDERSTANDING LIFE

The events of this time reveal that life's big questions, the enlightenment of the *conditio humana* in all its splendor and misery, are permanently relevant. We can approach the mystery of life from various perspectives. From our own experience, we know, first, that the span of our earthly, biological life is limited. For this reason, we need to contemplate both the start and the end of our earthly life, including our death. In view of this experience, we must ask questions about the source of life. According to Christian belief, God is the source of life because it is through him that "we live and move and have our being" (Acts 17:28).

From our understanding of God as the source of life, there are consequences for our behavior as individuals. To reach a holistic understanding of life, we need to look through God's eyes at the world and gaze up from the world toward God. Only through union with God does life make sense. Without a transcendent angle, human life is reduced to its own immanence, a brief biological life-span. Life is created by God, sustained by him, and preserved through his bountiful providence beyond the limits of our biological existence. All the autonomy, individuality, and subjectivity of the human person flow from this. The nature of the person as a created being is what defines their human existence.

According to biblical understanding, our lives are directed toward God and communion with him. This life in God and with God happens through our lives with others. All of life occurs in the living presence of God, including its beginning, the development of our lives as individuals, life's preservation, its limitation through death, and our hope of living communion beyond death. This is the total of life in its fullness.

God's promise is this life in fullness, and the human person, as a consecrated being, is invited during the span of their earthly life to live according to this promise. The fear of God and a living relationship with him is the basis of this right way to live. Even during the most dreadful catastrophes and experiences of pain, when our lives reach their breaking point, or even when those around us deny the presence of God or the existence of personal relationships with him, we may find refuge in God himself. This, even though God may permit hardships, which seem incomprehensible from our point of view (see Job 19:13–25).

If we seek to gain a proper understanding of human beings in the world, it is key that we are clear about the universal human inclination toward sin and our redemption through Jesus Christ. The existence of evil in the world is a universal human experience, and people are also trapped by the structures of evil. Humanity knows through experience that we are ambivalent beings: greatness and misery both being part of our sinful existence. The personal relationship between God and humanity made in his image can be lost through human sinfulness. In our freedom, we may choose to accept or reject a relationship with God. If we accept this, we will experience life in its fullness.

HOW TO LIVE IN THE FACE OF DEATH

The COVID-19 crisis has left us in a state of great anguish. For decades we have only looked at the positive side of life, burying its dark, negative aspects as far as possible. While living in a world of limitless opportunity, enthusiasm for technological possibilities, and a boundless euphoria for life, we have been unexpectedly plunged into the horror story of a pandemic. Suddenly, we realize that this could affect all of us personally, that we too could fall ill and die. In the face of death, human beings develop existential anxiety.

Our human fragility and fleeting existence have become starkly apparent. We are mortal. Death casts sharp light on the mystery of life. Facing the prospect of death, humanity itself becomes a question, as St. Augustine observed in a well-known phrase from his *Confessions*. Deep in pain over the unexpected death of a young friend, he remarked, "I have become a question to myself."[2]

Everyone consciously or unconsciously asks themselves the question, "What will happen when I die? What is the meaning of death?"[3] We know by experience that every human being born must die. Death thus belongs to life. It is part of our existence as humans, a fact that connects us to all other living creatures. We have the existential certainty that we must die. There is nothing so final as death itself; indeed, it is the most certain of all things in this world.

Death is invincible and final, which is why it is the crisis par excellence for humankind. We know about the death of others but try to bury all thought of our own demise. We simply don't want to think about it. Our personal knowledge of the death of others incites a natural temptation to save ourselves the bother of truly facing our own. However, to live a meaningful life, every one of us must confront—although painful—the unavoidable nature of death, the uncertainty of the hour, the final nature of the farewell. But obviously we are afraid of death, whether our own or that of our loved ones. The process of dying is surrounded with sorrow. All the pain, sorrow, and tears linked to death continue to be part of life itself. We cannot avoid this. Yet the path toward redemption consists of accepting death as a fact, with faith and in hope.

Against this backdrop of death and our mortal nature, the Christian faith proclaims that eternal life is a real possibility for us all. The basis of this faith is the resurrection of Jesus Christ. Upon this, the Christian faith stands or falls. "If Christ has not been raised, then our proclamation has been in vain and your faith has been in vain" (1 Cor 15:14). The resurrection of Jesus Christ is the basis for our hope for the resurrection of the dead, which is inseparably linked to the resurrection of Jesus: "But in fact Christ has been raised from the dead, the first fruits of those who have died. For since death came through a human being, the resurrection of the dead has also come through a human being" (1 Cor 15:20–21).

The hope of the resurrection of the dead presupposes the death and therefore mortal nature of humankind. We hope that death does not obliterate the identity of the dead. Resurrection in no way involves a new creation but rather a re-creation of this life. Eternal life is in substance no other life than this. It is our present life transformed.

> For this perishable body must put on imperishability, and this mortal body must put on immortality. When this perishable body puts on imperishability, and this mortal body puts on immortality, then the saying that is written will be fulfilled:
>
> "Death has been swallowed up in victory."
> "Where, O death, is your victory?
>   Where, O death, is your sting?"
>   (1 Cor 15:53–55)

In eternal life, the dead person is reborn, but their identity as an individual remains. Thus, resurrection means that God takes the whole person with the complete truth of their lives and personal story and transforms them until they stand transfigured, with nothing to hide in his presence. Death, therefore, only has the power to separate us from the earthbound part of human life. In contrast, resurrection makes visible the divine power of union. All that is human and of this earth is gathered into the eternal presence. The sundered body is made whole by the love of God and the disrupted life story is completed through his goodness. Eternal life is only the whole and final healing of our temporal mortal life: "So it is with the resurrection of the dead. What is sown is perishable, what is raised is imperishable. It is sown in dishonor, it is raised in glory. It is sown in weakness, it is raised in power. It is sown a physical body, it is raised a spiritual body. If there is a physical body, there is also a spiritual body" (1 Cor 15:42–44).

The Christian who believes in the resurrection of the dead is sustained by an unshakeable hope. We can live and love here and now, just as we can die with confidence, because of our assurance of being resurrected to eternal life.

Life, whose peak is eternal life, is based on the profound relationship of every mortal man and woman with God. The life-giving breath of God creates the relationship between God and his creatures, providing them with life and blessings. This relationship between God and humankind endures through life, the process of dying, and after death. Only God can withdraw his will from this relationship that he himself has established with his creatures. He will surely not do this, however, because he is faithful. When we use our freedom to also keep faith with God, we remain forever in this life-giving relationship with him. As mortal, perishable beings, we ourselves stay immortal and unperishable by virtue of this relationship—which may be mercifully redeemed, renewed, and transformed—as a created being with God.

Obviously, human life is transient in space and time, but the relationship between God and humanity has an eternal presence in God. We remain eternal in God and are immortal through him. As this communion with God is indestructible and through God remains eternal, through the power of God we can believe in eternal life. Thus, we can safely say that death marks the limit of our earthly life but not of God's relationship with us. In life and in death, God remains the Lord of life: "The Lord kills and brings to life; he brings down to Sheol and raises up" (1 Sam 2:6). Thus, death is but a door we go through. It transforms the earthbound nature of life: "Indeed for your faithful Lord, life is changed not ended, and, when this earthly dwelling turns to dust, an eternal dwelling is made ready for them in heaven."[4]

What can we do to ensure our life on earth is a success in the light of the promise of eternal life? Jesus invites us to receive his word with faith: "Very truly, I tell you, anyone who hears my word and believes him who sent me has eternal life, and does not come under judgment, but has passed from death to life" (John 5:24). It is an assurance of our faith that our Savior lives and we too shall live with him (see Job 19:25). Jesus Christ promises us, "I live, you also will live" (John 14:19). What he gives us is eternal life (see John 17:3).

The way to true life comprises the recognition and acceptance of the transcendent and eschatological dimension of human life. Our concern should be to acknowledge with faith, hope, and love this truth of the presence of God and his communion with us, so that we may let this develop form and substance in our lives. The primary goal of Christian life is knowledge of the Son of God (see Eph 4:13) because he is eternal life. We have life if we go to him and are with him: "Lord, to whom can we go? You have the words of eternal life" (John 6:68). If we build the foundations of our lives on Christ, we will receive life in its fullness. The Rule of St. Benedict recommends that we should prefer nothing to Christ, *Christo nihil omnino praeponere* (ch. 72, 11).

If we now regard life as a gift, then God in Christ is the giver. As giving is truly part of the essence of God, at the end of our lives, we will meet him as the giver. As a creature of God, I can trust that once my earthly life is over, my communion with him, who is life himself, will remain unbroken: "But if Christ is in you, though the body is dead because of sin, the Spirit is life because of righteousness. If the Spirit of him who raised Jesus from the dead dwells in you, he who raised Christ from the dead will give life to your mortal bodies also through his Spirit that dwells in you" (Rom 8:10–11).

Belief in life after death gives us the strength to look at life before death from a godly perspective and ensures that, through the power of God, it is a success. A Christian understands our earthly life as a pilgrimage to celestial glory. It is not a path of resignation but rather a dynamic journey made with our eyes fixed on heaven. To give a faith-filled yes to the promise of eternal life is the foundation that sustains our inner freedom and helps us to overcome the existential anxieties that tend to keep us blocked. Eternal life in Christ is our source of strength. The belief that this promise is already at work in us through the share we have received in the life of God revives within us an inner strength that allows us to have a life full of meaning. The hope that is alive in us motivates us time and again to tackle life with passion and gives us inner serenity despite all the challenges, suffering, burdens, and fears that overwhelm us.

When death is on the horizon or we are in a desperate situation, we find the strength to evaluate life with realism. Human beings are fragile; only God is eternal. Life, whether before or after death, is protected by the presence of God. If we accept this assurance in faith and trust we are in the hands of God, this will give us the strength of belief to survive even the most challenging of situations. This assurance is, in any case, a gift from God that we can ask for and expect to receive.

THE STRENGTH OF PRAYER IN TIMES OF NEED

In times of crisis, perhaps it is better if we speak less *of* God with others and more *with* God about the crisis. A Christian draws his or her strength fundamentally from prayer, from talking with God. We do not have strength on our own merit and therefore depend on the help of God. When in need, we cry out or sometimes even shout out to God. To cry out to God until he listens is an act of trust (see Ps 77:1).

> In the day of my trouble I seek the Lord;
>> in the night my hand is stretched out
>>> without wearying;
>> my soul refuses to be comforted. (Ps 77:2)

When in situations of unutterable suffering we lack words, we still have the option of remaining in silence before God.

Prayer is the natural attitude of the religious person, and this is especially true in situations of need and crisis. Prayer is not talking to oneself or to the wall. Prayer is a dialogue with God. It means speaking of love with the one who loves us, with whom we meet often and with pleasure (St. Teresa of Avila). For the praying person, God is their refuge:

> Therefore let all who are faithful
>   offer prayer to you;
> at a time of distress, the rush of mighty
>   waters
>   shall not reach them.
> You are a hiding place for me;
>   you preserve me from trouble;
>   you surround me with glad cries of
>   deliverance. (Ps 32:6–7)

Whoever prays with faith can rejoice in the help of the Lord: "You have seen my affliction; you have taken heed of my adversities" (Ps. 31:7). Even when God already knows our needs, we can still open our hearts to him with trust and show him our many wounds: "Into your hand I commit my spirit; you have redeemed me, O LORD, faithful God" (Ps 31:5). When there is an existential threat in the background, we can only ask God that we may learn to see and understand anew the ways of divine providence.

Through prayer, we express our existential dependence on God. This is fundamentally an avowal that the care and providence of God are always present, at any time, even in situations where the fruit of his love often remains unseen. *Although* and *yet* are words that express this basic attitude of trust:

Though the fig tree does not blossom,
  and no fruit is on the vines;
though the produce of the olive fails,
  and the fields yield no food;
though the flock is cut off from the fold,
  and there is no herd in the stalls,
yet I will rejoice in the Lord;
  I will exult in the God of my salvation.
GOD, the Lord, is my strength;
  he makes my feet like the feet of a deer,
  and makes me tread upon the heights.
    (Hab 3:17–19)

In the face of need and of death, we cannot, as religious people, fail to fix our gaze on the Lord and plead for his help. Our eyes look to heaven in supplication: "O Lord, I am oppressed; be my security!" (Isa 38:14). Prayer lets a new trust and hope grow within us.

Prayer is an act of trust, the path that brings us directly to the heart of God. It is the breath of the soul, our anchor in the many storms of life, as well as our consolation and guide. Prayer gives us the fortitude to enable us to overcome our existential fears and, confiding in God's paternal care, to live in trust and hope. The purpose of Jesus was to encourage people to entrust themselves to the goodness and care of the Father:

Therefore I tell you, do not worry about your life, what you will eat or what you will drink, or about your body, what you will wear. Is not life more than food, and the body more than clothing? Look at the birds of the air; they neither sow nor reap nor gather into barns, and yet your heavenly Father feeds them. Are you not of more value than they? And can any of you by worrying add a single hour to your span of life? (Matt 6:25–27)

As people who trust in God, we can praise God in times of joy, seek God in difficult times, worship and adore God in times of quietness, trust in God in times of crisis, and in all situations, give thanks to him.

At all times and in all situations, we are exhorted to take special care of our relationship with God through prayer. In the light of meaningless experiences, of sadness and fragility, we can accept with faith the words of the Gospel: "But to all who received him, who believed in his name, he gave power to become children of God" (John 1:12). As children of God, we can go to the Heavenly Father with all our anxieties: "Do not worry about anything, but in everything by prayer and supplication with thanksgiving let your requests be made known to God" (Phil 4:6).

Negative and positive experiences are both part of life: joy and sorrow accompany us our whole lives long. It is part of the law of life that we must die in order to live; the grain of wheat must die in order to live (see John 12:24). Without the cross, the Christian message is feeble and empty. While we live in the world, trials and tribulations are inevitable: "In the world you face persecution. But take courage; I have conquered the world!" (John 16:33). Yet when in our fear and necessity we look to Jesus and trust in his promise, he gives us the strength to cope with hardship and difficulties and to experience his consolation.

Throughout the history of Christianity, in situations of need, whether caused by epidemics, natural disasters, or war, believers have always regarded themselves as a praying community of faith. They have invoked the intercession of the saints, thus making visible and tangible the *communio sanctorum*, the Communion of Saints that we profess in the Creed. In times of crisis, believers have always prayed for those in dire need. This vicarious prayer for others expresses the fact we are one family in God. We need people to pray, we need intercessors and a community that expresses solidarity with others through prayer.

At the end of Lent, Pope Francis gave an inspiring example of intercessory prayer in the current crisis. The sight of the pope ascending the steps of St. Peter Square alone and praying in solitude between the Crucifix of San Marcello, which had been carried through Rome during the 1522 plague outbreak, and an icon of Our Lady Salus Populi Romani, before he finally imparted a blessing to the world with the blessed sacrament, is an image that will remain ingrained in the collective memory of this century.

A NEW LIFESTYLE
AFTER THE CRISIS

The COVID-19 crisis could become a wake-up call for an age whose normal focus is on worldly ideas. Our thoughts fixate on seeking various earthly paradises to satisfy our longings. We talk nowadays of idyllic holidays or places, surfing or shopping paradises, tax havens, and so on. Nowadays people live and work hard relentlessly, neglecting to rest, so they can access these types of paradise.

Most people have images of paradise, regardless of their culture and religion. We must go beyond such ideas, which are, for the most part, confined to this world, in order to arrive at a true, holistic understanding of the human person: "Do not be conformed to this world, but be transformed by the renewing of your minds, so that you may discern what is the will of God—what is good and acceptable and perfect" (Rom 12:2). This is only possible if we stop fixating on the here and now and broaden our horizons to focus on heaven, so that the whole of our lives may be lived out in fullness.

Only with a perspective changed by faith can we reach the real heaven that awaits us at the end of our lives. It is filled with the presence of God who grants us final salvation, fulfillment, and happiness. This is a paradise that cannot be "made": it belongs to God alone. The path toward heaven is typified by a temperate lifestyle, in which we deny our selfish inclinations and avoid self-destructive behavior that destroys relationships and the lives of others.

In the light of the variety and number of possible natural disasters, we must again admit just how little we really know about nature and the world we live in. COVID-19 has shown us how interconnected the world is and that we are all one community, bound to the same fate. We have become newly aware of the unity binding God and humanity, that we are one universal fraternity. What is clear from this is our need to care for our common home and live in universal solidarity.[5] Every single individual and humanity as a whole is called to a conversion and complete renewal of the heart, so that we may commit to creating a credible human ecology.[6]

Changing our lifestyle will help us to develop the capacity to go out of ourselves towards the other. Unless we do this, other creatures will not be recognized for their true worth; we are unconcerned about caring for things for the sake of others; we fail to set limits on ourselves in order to avoid the suffering of others or the deterioration of our surroundings. Disinterested concern for others, and the rejection of every form of self-centeredness and self-absorption, are essential if we truly wish to care for our brothers and sisters and for the natural environment. These attitudes also attune us to the moral imperative of assessing the impact of our every action and personal decision on the world around us. If we can overcome individualism, we will truly be able to develop a different lifestyle and bring about significant changes in society.[7]

True knowledge of God and realistic self-knowledge lead directly to empathy and solidarity with our fellow human beings and to a praxis of compassion.

In this time of crisis, the anagram *COVID* has become ingrained in our memories. *COVID*, denoting the sickness triggered by the coronavirus, may ultimately provide us with ethical and spiritual guidance for our lifestyle during and after the pandemic.

C: Confidence (Trust in God)

O: Opportunities (To be seized)

V: Values (Rediscovery of our core values)

I: Intelligence (The wisdom to discern spirits)

D: Devotion (Surrendering to God on behalf of humankind and the world)

GOD HAS THE LAST WORD

The COVID-19 pandemic and our ensuing fears about the future will pass, just as other awful episodes in the history of the world have also passed before. We can trust in the care and providence of God not only in this pandemic, but in all natural disasters and all our personal fortunes, even when times seem sad and painful. As fragile beings, through faith we can learn to accept our own limitations and entrust our sense of powerlessness to God: "We are afflicted in every way, but not crushed; perplexed, but not driven to despair" (2 Cor 4:8).

For Thomas, it was in the wounds of Christ that he experienced the risen Lord (see John 20:24–29). Might the wounds of this pandemic give us an opportunity to have a new experience of God? If we believers trustingly bring our own frailty and that of our fellow human beings, plus the need we all share for redemption into God's plan of salvation for the whole of creation, then a new strength will rise up within us. Through the strength of faith we can cry out to our fear-stricken world with St. John Paul II: "Do not be afraid. Open wide the doors for Christ!"[8] Christ the Savior can heal us. He is the Redeemer and the Savior of the world. He alone is our hope.

In the light of life's many threats and dangers, each of us, according to what is feasible, has the mission through the power of our faith to help advance the complete, sustainable development of the whole human family. As Christians, we should always remember the weak and needy, the poor and the sick, and do everything possible to alleviate and eliminate their needs and suffering. To do this, we may draw strength from our living relationship with God. He is a God who is for us and a God who walks with us. He remains with us all the days of our life (see Exod 3:14; Matt 28:20). He has not abandoned us at this time either. His healing and saving presence are a certainty and source of strength for those who believe.

As Christians we live on hope. Death only has the penultimate word: God himself has the last word, which is resurrection, life in its fullness, and eternal life. If we rely on the faithfulness of God and trust in him, we will reach a reassuring certainty: we humans do not have everything under control, but we are in God's hands. The Christian does not shape their own life through their own power, but rather through the power of the Holy Spirit. In uncertain times, we can entrust ourselves fully to his guidance. Through the Spirit's gift of wisdom, we can accept life, and shape it through the options open to us as well as through its limitations. Through the gift of wisdom, we can learn to appreciate, care for, and preserve life in all its holiness and beauty. Through the gift of insight, we can choose to make the right decisions whenever necessary. Through the gift of fear of the Lord, we can develop deep reverence for life and for creation and live out a spirit of universal humanity through our love for humankind.

Our faith may be tested and questioned not only by the current crisis but by many other global and localized disasters. Yet this should not lead us to despair but rather to growing strength and certainty in our faith and a deeper realization that God is the Lord and ruler of history, past, present, and future. He can lead us through any crisis. In his hands we are kept safe. At a time where the whole of humanity suffers under the threat of the pandemic, our faith can provide us with hope and trust. The power of faith is the strength that conquers the power of fear. In the light of this severe trial and suffering, not only related to this pandemic, but to all natural disasters, we, as believers may identify existentially with the words of this well-known poem by the German theologian, Dietrich Bonhoeffer:

> By gracious pow'rs so wonderfully sheltered,
> and confidently waiting come what may,
> We know that God is with us night and
>   morning
> And never fails to greet us each new day.[9]

Notes

1. St. Augustine, Sermon 52, 6.

2. St. Augustine, *Confessions*, IV, 4, 9.

3. For further thoughts on the topic of death, immortality and eternal life, see J. Ratzinger, *Eschatologie: Tod und ewiges Leben* (Regensburg: Pustet, 1977); Eng. trans.: *Eschatology: Death and Eternal Life* (Washington, DC: The Catholic University of America Press, 1988); J. Pieper, *Tod und Unsterblichkeit*, ed. Berthold Wald (Kevelaer: Gemeinschaft, 2012); Eng. trans.: *Death and Immortality* (New York: Herder, 1969).

4. Roman Missal, Preface No. 1 for the Dead.

5. See Pope Francis's encyclical *Laudato Si'*, On Care for Our Common Home.

6. See *Laudato Si'*, 5.

7. *Laudato Si'*, 208.

8. With this hope-filled cry, John Paul II began his pontificate on October 16, 1978.

9. *Gotteslob: Katholisches Gebet-und Gesangbuch* (Stuttgart, 2013), 430; Eng. trans.: *The United Methodist Hymnal* (Carol Stream, IL: Hope Publishing, 1974).

CHAPTER 3

DISTANCE AND CONTACT

CHARITY RESPECTS, AND OVERCOMES, BOUNDARIES

THOMAS SÖDING

Charity is the hallmark of biblical ethics. It has become a very special kind of world heritage. Based in the Old Testament (Lev 19:18), Jesus joins it with the love for God, puts it front and center (Mark 12:28–34 par.), and spreads it far beyond Christendom with the parable of the Good Samaritan (Luke 10:25–37). Paul saw charity as the fulfillment of the law (Gal 5:13–14; Rom 13:8–10). According to the Epistle of James, charity characterizes the royal freedom of all Christians (Jas 2:8). According to the First Epistle of John, charity—toward the sister, toward the brother—is the essential criterion of an authentic love for God (1 John 4:20).

Charity is an ethic on equal terms and within sight. It is not condescending but humble, not patronizing but emphatic. It does not venture out into the distance but goes near. It is an affair of the heart—or it is not charity.

THE QUESTION OF PROXIMITY

The critical question is, To whom do people open their heart? And to whom do they shut it? Whom do people allow to draw close? And to whom do they want to be close? Whom do they view as their neighbor? Whom do they ignore? By whom do they want to be seen as neighbor? And by whom rather not?

The realism of these questions strengthens charity as an ethical principle. Charity qualifies responsibility. It requires prioritizing in the face of limited resources. It develops a dynamic in the spirit of Jesus, not to deny the boundaries of religion, nation, morals, and interest, but to transcend them in order to see neighbors as the people they are for the faithful in the eyes of God: creatures to whom God in his love grants the gift of life; brothers and sisters of Jesus, who shares their life; weak creatures that are meant to be strengthened; sinful creatures in need of redemption; and images of God that are destined for eternal life. Charity is a broad intersection between anthropology and ethics.

The times of COVID-19 sharpen the focus of these questions: How can human closeness be designed as an expression of love and not of exuberance or thoughtlessness? How much distance does proximity require? And how much proximity does distance require? Which contacts do not infect but heal? Which boundaries does charity respect and guard, which ones become permeable—and how? Where do we find God in these processes? And which forms of charity open and fulfill themselves in the love for God? The quarantine and its transcendence are a case of emergency for charity.[1]

THE QUALITY OF RELATIONSHIPS

Charity is an expression of personal ethics. Political ethics works differently, first and foremost according to the principle of justice. Aristotle explained the principle in the fifth book of his *Nicomachean Ethics*[2]—which needs to be explained again and again.[3] Justice and love are not opposed but they stand in tension to each other.[4] No state can love in the sense of the biblical *agape*, only a person can do so: God can love, humans can love. It is precisely that which joins the love for God with the love for your neighbor—both are, according the Bible, based upon the love of God itself.

The commandment of charity describes the person of the neighbor clearly. The Old Testament names the "fellow countryman," the "brother," and the "child" of the same people (Lev 19:16–18). The programmatic expansion to the "alien" (Lev 19:34) living under a sort of protection in the land for some time without being Jewish shows that this description is meant positively, not exclusively. The commandment focuses on those with whom one is actually dealing: within one's neighborhood, one's quarter, at work, in the marketplace. Martin Buber nails it when he interprets that it brings the focus to "people with whom you are dealing in the course of your life."[5] The examples mentioned to characterize the test of charity make it clear that it is especially demanded in conflict situations, and from those who would have good reason to feel hurt, dismissed, or disadvantaged. We are to overcome hate through *correctio fraterna*, and not cede any ground to desires for revenge.

The tradition of the New Testament broadens this horizon further—without obliterating the point of the commandment—to put the focus where encounters and challenges occur within one's plain view, area of activity and area of responsibility. Three factors promote this opening. First, the sociological and historical context has significantly changed compared to the history of the people of Israel as imagined in the law of holiness (Lev 14—26), both through the presence of Gentiles in Galilee and Judea in the times of Jesus (see Matt 8:5–13 par.; Luke 7:1–10) and through the universal mission of early Christendom (see 1 Thess 4:1–12). Second, both Jesus's homily on the kingdom of God and the faith in his resurrection from the dead open a eschatological perspective, which also characterizes ethics because it increases the appreciation of earthly life (Mark 8:35 par.; Phil 1:12–26) as well as the hope for an eternal life beyond despair and death (Mark 14:25 par.; Rom 14:7–9). Third, Jesus verifies in his practice and teaching that even the suffering of brutal aggression, exploitation, and oppression is not a reason not to see enemies as people that are meant to become neighbors, even if it costs money and willpower, demands willingness to suffer, and the taking of the first step, the second step, and the third step toward reconciliation, even where the other is in the wrong (Matt 5:38–48 par.; Luke 6:27–36). The decisive reason is theological: God himself loves his enemies; he grants them life; he does not mistake their deeds and misdeeds; but he opens them a perspective if they repent. Paul emphasizes in his doctrine of justification that this love of God is not just a chance for the others, the evil, the criminal, but for oneself—the only justification for a life in the freedom of the faith and in the hopes of completion (Rom 5:5).[6]

But the commandment of love does not merely benefit the neighbor; it strengthens the person that is meant to exercise charity in three ways. First: "*Thou* shalt love"—this is about the person themselves, not about any other person that might jump in. Second: "Thou shalt love *thy* neighbor"—not anyone, one's own environment is important, personal responsibility. Third: "Thou shalt love thy neighbor *as thyself*"—beyond egoism, but also beyond self-destruction, within a humanness that finds fulfillment in the service for others, without exploiting that for the purpose of self-discovery. The humanity of charity is grounded in this tripartite personality.

The word *agape* characterizes the quality of the relationship.[7] It is a discovery by the Septuagint, the translation of the Hebrew Bible into Greek, the lingua franca back then. The *Biblia Graeca* defines as *agape* those forms of love that are marked by God himself as worshiped in Israel. He loves his people—especially the pious, the just, and the wise. The love of the people of Israel is to respond to his love: undivided, faithful, from all of their heart, with all of their life and with all within their power (Deut 6:4–5). To this love for God correspond the love for the neighbor and the stranger and, according to Jesus, the enemy.

The British author C. S. Lewis distinguished this form of love, *agape*, from other forms of love, without separating it from them.[8] He follows the Greek language, which is especially rich in differentiation. Greek knows *eros* as desire that unleashes enormous power and creativity but also always reveals a want, which is why Plato calls it a demon. It knows friendship (*philia*) as a close exchange characterized by voluntariness that promotes communality between two people or within a small group. It also knows the love between parents and children (*storgé*) as a natural inclination manifesting itself in caring, the fostering of their relationship and a reliable connection, even if today's sociology and anthropology focus strongly on the cultural imprint on the natural.

Agape can enter into close relationship with all of these forms of love. But it does not dissolve itself in them. It is independent. Even more: it is original because it is founded in God and given by him. *Agape* is a creative love. It says yes to the other, to God, and to the neighbor. It does not content itself in saying, I love you the way you are. *Agape* says, I love you because you are.

In his first encyclical *Deus Caritas Est*, Benedict XVI took up this theology of love.[9] He defended it against a strain of thinking common in the West, that the love for God is irreconcilable with self-love.[10] He showed how within the love for God we find an ethic of charity that recognizes in the other the person that God loves like oneself, so that in the service for others we fulfill ourselves in a way that very much responds to human rationality.

THE ETHICS OF DISTANCE

Not only COVID-19 containment strategies have led to a new recognition of the ethical importance of distance and distancing. The medical discussion focuses on triage,[11] access to medication, operating rooms, and protective gear.

The political debate focuses on the relationship between freedom and security.[12]

The ethical questions on a personal level, which are the focus of the commandment to love, reach further. They have rediscovered the meaning of distance through two powerful societal developments: for one, the Me Too movement[13] condemning sexual harassment, especially by men, worldwide. Keeping distance respects sexual self-determination, limits the temptation of power, and creates in the first place the condition for a cooperative, friendly, and collegial relationship. The Catholic Church has been challenged by the sexual abuse scandal.

In addition, the political, social, cultural, and peda-gogical discourse has recognized heterogeneity as a basic category. In this development, processes of communica-tion do not lead to sublime appropriations, but recognize and accept others as such, so that they can be promoted in a way that allows them to communicate freely from their own standpoint and to develop self-determination.[14]

Both modern movements connect with ancient *topoi* of justice and ethics: with the respect for privacy,[15] with data protection in the analog and digital worlds[16]—at their core with the respect for the freedom of the others, who themselves must not transgress, but who have the plain right to develop their personality. Discretion, more than just confidentiality, is a basic premise of pastoral theology we should rediscover: the differentiation that enables action and judgment because it is willing to a keep a safe distance.

The commandment of charity does not impede but expands liberty, which needs protection against infringe-ment.[17] At its base it establishes that the neighbor is *not* oneself so as to become visible, important, equal, challenging, irritating, and enriching merely thereby. Whoever makes their neighbor their alter ego extends help as sublime egoism. The anthropology of charity especially reveals the perversion behind such a rationalization, however often it may occur, however much it may be mingled with altruistic motives. The New Testament clearly warns us of encroaching upon others even in purported benevolence. The First Epistle of Peter combines an encouragement to the disciples to bear witness to their new hope with the exhortation to only do so with "gentleness and reverence" (1 Pet 3:16).

The dialogical relationship unleashed by the commandment to love means that self-protection is a commandment of charity as much as is the protection of the other from too much love, which can stifle and then is anything but love in the sense of the Torah and Jesus. For police and first responders, self-protection is an ethical standard assured by laws and regulations.[18] It is based on the idea that nobody can be forced into martyrdom and that everybody needs to ensure their ability to help others. From a theological perspective, self-love is based in the knowledge of being loved by God. Life, terrestrial and celestial, is invaluable (Mark 8:36–37). Hope for eternal life neither justifies laissez-faire nor contempt for the world, but entails responsibility and compassion—something proven by Christian free spirits such as Catherine of Siena and ascetics like Antonius—because it is the God to whom we look for that very redemption, the Creator, that brings to life this world every moment anew, because he loves it. That is why in the spirit of charity nobody must place themselves unnecessarily in danger. Granted, *in extremis* one might decide to sacrifice one's life for another's, as did Maximilian Kolbe in a concentration camp when he saved a father's life by dying in his stead,[19] but that is an entirely different matter. The freedom to walk in the path of the cross until the end (Mark 8:34 par.) is the flip side of the freedom not to throw away one's life. Both are expressed in the love we experience from God and that we pass on.

Inasmuch as the protection of one's own person is important in charity, it is even more important not to endanger another person through one's own acts, however lofty the ethical ends. The Torah, in the logic of its time, explains that quarantine can be a commandment by God (Lev 13—14). Leprosy was seen as uncleanliness that spreads through bodily contact.[20] There was neither vaccination nor medication against it, so that a pandemic could only be stopped by prohibiting contact. Christian exegesis has often presented those rules as an expression of typical Old Testament cruelty—and unjustly so. Jesus himself, as messianic Son of God, does not need to fear contagion and, as the Gospels show, can heal the leprous (Mark 1:40–45 par.; Luke 17:11–19); but he ensures that they present themselves to the responsible priests, who have medical knowledge, so that they might receive a medical attestation.

Now Jesus indeed promised to his disciples in his typical metaphorical clarity in Luke 10:19 that they can even step on scorpions and snakes without being harmed as they propagate the gospel,[21] because they cannot be beaten by evil and can even drive out demons (see Luke 10:17). But he did not recommend imprudence and recklessness. The New Testament reports healings of leprosy by Jesus, but not by the apostles. The Apocrypha are very reserved as well in that respect and such reservation is smart. Only the emergence of medicine enables treatment.

We can see a Christian way of dealing with leprosy, which took on new forms because of a change of
circumstances, by looking at two people of the modern
era. Damian de Veuster, canonized in 2009, was active in
the treatment and pastoral care of lepers on the island
of Moloka'i for a long time and with great devotion and
prudence—and he finally was infected so that he died of
leprosy in 1889.[22] Albert Schweitzer, on the other hand, as
the "jungle doctor" of the town of Lambarene, acquired
great merit in fighting the disease and sensitizing people
for both treatment options and actions of solidarity.[23] Both
men ethically promoted distance and closeness—with different consequences because of different times.

The example of the healing of lepers, back then in
the gospel of Jesus and today in modern medicine, international health politics, and sustainable prophylaxis by
good nourishment and education, demonstrates two
things. First: the Church is not Jesus; the Church is not
God. It is weak and vulnerable; it can be infected and
infect others.[24] Second: the disciples are agents of Christ.
In their weakness, their limitations, their own endanger-
ment, they can and should help—and respect those limitations that are not within their power to change.

Keeping this balance was and is important when
practicing charity. It was right that, in a time that lacked
local and governmental structures, and far into the modern age, the Church, similar to other organizations and
religions, itself built leprosy homes for the purpose of
isolation and the protection of others, which also enabled
pastoral care for the sick.[25] And so it is important today,
when it promotes sustainable development and mini-
mizes risk with charity organizations such as Caritas,
Misereor, Adveniat, Missio, and Renovabis.

The Church, too, is under the ethical imperative, for the purpose of charity, to respect and promote the rules of distancing, which, in times of plague, are based on science. From a New Testament perspective, the Church has no sacral right not to respect ethical standards. The idea that nobody could suffer an infection during the Mass or from the receipt of the sacraments reveals magical thinking. Paul thought differently. He reminds the Corinthians that while the exodus generation took the manna (Exod 16:4–35; Ps 78:24–25) and drank the water from the rock (Exod 17:6; Num 20:7–11; Ps 78:15–16) as spiritual food and drink, it still danced around the golden calf (1 Cor 10:1–14). A few sentences on, he castigates the Corinthians for, on the one hand, celebrating the Eucharist in memory of Jesus Christ, and on the other hand, disavowing it by their social behavior in humbling the poor, who were not fully allowed to participate in the breaking of the bread, which in those times did not only consist of the Eucharist but also of a (not yet so-called) *agape* feast (1 Cor 11:17–34). Both go together. The Church should not engage in sacramentalism, but it should take the connection of liturgy and charity to heart. A celebration that spreads the plague is out of place. But when it respects and permeates boundaries, it is effective as a sacrament.

THE PERMEABILITY OF BOUNDARIES

Charity has and knows boundaries and limitations; but it also does a lot to overcome them: the Samaritan, a brother, who should be the hereditary enemy, turns into an example (Luke 10:25–37). A sinner, in washing Jesus's feet with her tears and hair and anointing them with oil, shows in her love the meaning of a healing faith (Luke 7:36–50). The adulteress is not sentenced to death, neither actually nor symbolically, but called to new life (John 8:1–11). People can become neighbors who as pagans seemed unclean but whom God himself proved clean (Acts 10). We are to win over an enemy by doing good (Rom 12:9–21). The poor are not to sit in the back but in the front of the church (Jas 2). We could continue this chain. It is not specifically from the New Testament, as if in opposition to the Old Testament, but takes up the universal dynamism that is based on the universal holiness of God (Lev 19:1–2) and marks both the love of the neighbor (Lev 19:18) and of the stranger (Lev 19:34). Jesus translated that dynamism into his own time and turned it into pastoral practice by his own mission and by the mission he gave to his disciples—first for Israel and, following Easter, for all peoples.

Love is the moral energy of transcendence. It connects heaven and earth: from God and to God. It renders earthly boundaries permeable that may have been set by governments, social injustice, gender roles, ecological catastrophes, or even by religious conviction or cultural tradition.

So how do boundaries that are not only set for charity, but also by charity, become permeable without endangering people in life and limb?

A theological response to the most important question raised by the pandemic would not make any sense if it didn't involve God. But any reflection *sub specie Dei* would amount to hubris if it wasn't clear about being a human response, about being under the eschatological condition that while it may well recognize the image of God in the world's mirror, that image is dark and unclear, the clear image remaining reserved for the final days, as Paul says in his "Ode to Love" (1 Cor 13:12).

Looking at the gospel and the entire New Testament, we see time and again that crossing boundaries is not a unilateral but a bilateral affair. Certainly: God helps, in the person of Jesus, and only he can help if death is to be made permeable for life, misery for redemption, hate for love—in the dimensions of a new creation.

But using a theology of grace, it would be a huge mistake with fatal consequences for the ethics of distance and contact to only consider God's actions at and for humanity and not also God's actions within, with, and through humanity that are based thereupon. Because the ethics of charity demand reciprocity. They take the initiative to show solidarity and mercy. Humans can be in a situation that is both physically and mentally so difficult that they need to be protected from themselves, and it requires sound judgment whether they would have acted the same way had they been free. But nobody can be forced into their own happiness. Otherwise charity would no longer be charity, but imperiousness. Therefore, one's own actions are ethically well-founded only when they are wanted by the other and trigger a reaction of the other that does not perpetuate dependence but promotes independence. Now the question is how such reciprocity can, theologically, be seen and practiced as love.

The story of Jesus responds to this question in manifold ways. Jesus's healings are typical in that they express his compassion (Mark 10:46–47 par.), his love, which commiserates and wants to help, and can. The gospel is clear that Jesus takes the first step when he announces that the kingdom of heaven is near (Mark 1:15). But typically Jesus becomes effective through the words "your faith has made you well" (Mark 10:52 par.; see Mark 5:34 par.; Luke 17:10—with a Samaritan). This is also the redeeming formula when he forgives the sins of the woman anointing him (Luke 7:50). Faith[26] in the Bible is a comprehensive, all-encompassing response to God, uniting trust and action, cognition, and creed. Such faith can only be personal, in the first person singular and plural. It would not be faith if it didn't have a counterpart—a "you"—in mind, even if that "you" is as invisible as God. The basic formula of a creed is "I believe in you."[27] Faith overcomes the boundaries between sickness and health and between guilt and forgiveness—by the love of Jesus, to which a faith responds that itself is a love relationship to Jesus.

In the young Church, a faith trusting in God's love connects Jews and Greeks, slaves and free, men and women. They remain what they are: humans; they become what they are: humans. Faith does not dissolve their identities, but the power of grace overcomes social discrimination and creates a new unity. That unity is celebrated in love (Gal 3:26–28).

Today's hermeneutics of faith poses the question of how not only liturgy but also catechism and the Church's public welfare institutions (*diakonie*) can build the dialectics of proximity and distance. The New Testament cannot deliver the final response but rather food for thought. Faith finds expression in prayer,[28] prayer is recognition, praise, gratitude, solicitation, and lamentation. In all of these types of prayer the faithful do not only bring their own wishes before God, but those of the whole world: in intercessions, in the praise for God by the people he delivered (Rom 11:33–36), in gratitude for the gift of life (Rom 8:31–39), in the lamentation expressing the silent outcry of the tormented creature (Rom 8:16–30). There is great longing for these prayers; to satisfy it is an imperative of charity, which is a sister to the love for God. The Church has manifold possibilities to tailor its prayers to the crisis in order to make it permeable for God, whom people miss and search; but how well it uses them is different from place to place.

The depth of the catechism, the propagation, the ministry must match the breadth of liturgy. This theological enlightenment is an imperative of charity as well. Many people are waiting for interpretation; and it shall open the eyes and hearts of those who act in the name of the Church. Any theological reflection on the crisis has at least three aspects. First, the dimensions of the crisis are estimated correctly: the pandemic, on the one hand, is not the apocalypse but a worldly phenomenon that can be limited in its effects and can be overcome in many of its negative consequences, by decisive, correct, and effective action; on the other hand, it is not merely an accident in the world's gearing mechanism, but a trial that must turn into an individual and collective soul-searching, and a wake-up call that prompts searching for new forms of responsible living in security and liberty. Second, it stimulates and reorients ethics. The pandemic is a case of emergency in ethical decision-making. In the midst of all economic, social, and medical considerations, it is necessary to respect the dignity of all humans, irrespective of their age, health, or national origin. That requires worldwide solidarity, which always begins locally.[29] It is necessary to define proximity, which has either already been realized or is yet to be created, and establishes responsibility without overchallenging. As this orientation becomes clearer, it strengthens the motivation that lies within faith. Third, one looks to the consolation in faith, in theology, to express people's grief, sorrow, and fear during the pandemic and to provide them with consolation in a hope for eternal life that does not deny the ephemeral but enlightens it.

Finally, *diakonie* is required. The Church as a not-for-profit organization is active in fulfilling public needs, in health care, care for the sick, social work with children and youth, and education. Everywhere the Church's activity depends on the political and social context; where it becomes active, it has no privilege but must prove itself through its service, its responsibility, and also through its attitude. Furthermore, personal encounter is required, from telephonic pastoral care to palliative care, and from help for families to refugee work. A lot is being done—but mostly in the shadows, without being honored appropriately. A lot yet needs to be done—mostly locally, where charity becomes concrete.

Charity respects boundaries because those who practice it know their own faults and entrust them to God, at least in their lucid moments. Charity crosses boundaries because it is love—even if it takes its distances in order to protect others, and places its trust in God, who hopefully will be infinitely near where no human can reach the other.

Notes

1. See Katharina Klöcker, "Gott in der Krise finden," *Herder Korrespondenz* 74, no. 5 (2020): 32–34.

2. Aristotle, *Nikomachische Ethik*, trans. Olaf Gigon (Düsseldorf, 2001).

3. Especially influential today: John Rawls, "Justice as Fairness," in *A Theory of Justice* (Cambridge, MA: Harvard University Press, 2001).

4. See Paul Ricoeur, *Liebe und Gerechtigkeit—Amour et Justice*, with a German parallel translation by M. Raden, ed. Oswald Bayer (Tübingen, 1990).

5. *Zwei Glaubensweisen* (1950), in Martin Buber, *Werke I* (München-Heidelberg, 1962), 651–782, at 701–2.

6. On the ecumenical doctrine of justification, see "The Biblical Foundations of the Doctrine of Justification: An Ecumenical Follow-Up to the Joint Declaration on the Doctrine of Justification," presented by a task force of biblical scholars and systematic theologians from the Lutheran World Federation, the Pontifical Council for Promoting Christian Unity, the World Communion of Reformed Churches, and the World Methodist Council, Geneva 2011.

7. See Oda Wischmeyer, *Liebe als Agape. Das frühchristliche Konzept und der moderne Diskurs* (Tübingen, 2016).

8. See Clive Staples Lewis, *The Four Loves: Affection–Friendship–Eros–Charity* (Glasgow, 1960).

9. Benedict XVI, encyclical *Deus Caritas Est*.

10. Prominently argued by Anders Nygren, *Eros und Agape. Gestaltwandlung der christlichen Liebe III* (Gütersloh, 1957).

11. See Alexander Brech, *Triage und Recht: Patientenauswahl beim Massenanfall Hilfebedürftiger in der Katastrophenmedizin*, Contributing to the Health Justice Debate (Berlin, 2008).

12. See Hinnerk Wißmann, "Was kommt nach dem Shutdown? Sicherheit vs. Freiheit," *FAZ*, April 8, 2020.

13. See Abby Ohlheiser, "The Woman behind *Me Too* Knew the Power of the Phrase When She Created It—10 Years Ago," *Washington Post*, October 19, 2017.

14. Adopted for the field of religious education: von Bernhard Grümme, "Religionspädagogische Denkformen.

Eine kritische Revision im Kontext von Heterogenität"
(QD 299) (Freiburg i. Br., 2019).

15. See Beate Rössler, *Der Wert des Privaten* (Frankfurt a. M., 2001).

16. See Marie-Theres Tinnefeld, Benedict Buchner, and Thomas Petri, *Einführung in das Datenschutzrecht. Datenschutz und Informationsfreiheit in europäischer Sicht* (München, 2012).

17. The relationship between freedom and love as mutual encouragement and destiny goes back to the Apostle Paul; see Gal 5:1–13.

18. See Thomas Mentzel, Isabel Schmitt-Falckenberg, and Kirsten Wischnewski, *Eigensicherung und Recht* (Munich, 2003).

19. See Andreas Murk and Konrad Schlattmann, *Maximilian Kolbe. Märtyrer der Nächstenliebe* (Würzburg, 2011).

20. See Christian Frevel, ed., *Purity and the Forming of Religious Traditions in the Ancient Mediterranean World and Ancient Judaism* (Leiden, 2013).

21. See Benedict T. Viviano, "The Return of the Seventy (Luke 10:17–20)," in *Il verbo di Dio è vivo*, ed. Aguilar Chiu and José Enrique, New Testament Studies in Honor of Cardinal Albert Vanhoye, SI, AnBib 165 (Rome: 2007), 219–23.

22. See Gavan Daws and Damian De Veuster, *Den Aussätzigen ein Aussätziger geworden*, with an afterword by Christian Feldmann (Freiburg im Breisgau, 1988).

23. See Albert Schweitzer, *Gesammelte Werke I: Aus meinem Leben und Denken; Aus meiner Kindheit und Jugendzeit; Zwischen Wasser und Urwald; Briefe aus Lambarene 1924–1927* (Munich, 1974).

24. Tomáš Halík, "Christentum in Zeiten der Krankheit," *Münster Forum for Theology and Church* 2, April 2020, emphasizes, "The plague shows that the world is sick and that the Church is a 'field hospital' (a metaphor of Pope Francis). But Corona also reveals the world as a sanatorium—and the Church as vulnerable. To many, it seems superfluous. The pandemic reinforces tendencies that would exist even without it. Theology is still more important."

25. Stefan Winkle's *Kulturgeschichte der Seuchen* provides an overview (Düsseldorf-Zürich, 1997).

26. See Jörg Frey et al., eds., *Glaube. Das Verständnis des Glaubens im frühen Christentum und in seiner jüdischen und hellenistisch-römischen Umwelt*, WUNT 373 (Tübingen, 2017).

27. Thus the basic definition in Joseph Ratzinger, *Einführung in das Christentum. Vorlesungen über das Apostolische Glaubensbekenntnis* (Tübingen, 1968), 57–59.

28. See Hans Klein, Vasile Mihoc, and Karl-Wilhelm Niebuhr, eds., *Das Gebet im Neuen Testament*, WUNT 249 (Tübingen, 2010).

29. See Franz-Josef Overbeck, "Niemandem mehr abverlangen, als für das Gemeinwohl notwendig ist," *The World* 7, May 2020.

CHAPTER 4

EXPERIENCING COVID-19 IN NEW YORK CITY

*Mark-David Janus, CSP**

This is my story of surviving the COVID-19 virus. It is one story among many, each with different configurations of symptoms, bodily responses, access to medical care. There are hundreds of thousands of stories people have not lived to tell. Their stories must be told by the grieving loved ones left behind.

My story begins with the COVID-19 virus attacking quickly, without warning, within hours rendering me helpless. Living in New York City, it should not have been unexpected. Ominous news reports warned the virus was coming: first to China, then Europe, Seattle, and it was just a matter of time—to New York City. People prepared as if a blizzard was coming, laying in extra groceries for a long weekend. It was more contagious than other viruses, even able to be transmitted

*Rev. Mark-David Janus, CSP, PhD, is the president and publisher of Paulist Press.

by people without symptoms, so people began to work from home. The New York St. Patrick's Day parade was canceled. Sporting events, concerts, operas, ballet, even Broadway theaters went dark, all social events postponed until the storm passed.

I had a persistent cold, but went to bed unconcerned, relaxed, eager for tomorrow. Within a few hours, I awoke with fever, chills, sweat, and constant thirst. My rib cage, front and back ached, the top of my head hurt. I lost control of bodily functions. I lost track of time—days blended, exhaustion created confusion—and then came delirium. I had no idea what day it was, I had no idea a week had passed, nor did I care. I cared only about finding a posture that would allow me to rest without hurting. My religious community[1] called a doctor who made a special house call to examine me. He was confident I had the virus, but I could not be tested because there were no tests to be had. There was no specific treatment, and, since I wasn't gasping for breath and my blood pressure was reasonable, I would be treated at home, placed in absolute quarantine, and given medications to reduce my symptoms. If my breathing became more painful, I would need immediate hospitalization.

During the first week of my illness, I did not think about living or dying, nor did I think about getting better. I was too exhausted to be anxious. My body, focused on escaping pain and coping with fever, had no time for consciousness or fear. Time was measured only by sensations of sickness, brief respites of sleep, and the gift of delirium that allowed escape. I did not understand what my body was doing. There was no energy for prayer.

In the second week of the illness, I was fortunate. The medications provided enough symptom relief to allow me sleep. The virus began to work its way out of my body without the crushing shortness of breath that sent people to the hospital or grave. My religious community made it possible for me to devote the little energy I had to healing. I did not have to worry about providing for myself or my family. I did not have to worry about losing my job. The truly saintly religious sisters[2] at the rectory would call me at mealtimes, offer encouragement, prepare food my system could tolerate, and leave it outside my quarantined room.

As symptoms abated, my self-awareness grew, and with it, recognition that I was not alone. Increasingly, I was aware of those protecting me. Through the sacrament of my cell phone, people anointed me with daily text messages, breaking the quarantine with care, concern, love, and always prayer—assurances, promises, guarantees of prayer. Emails transformed into the angelic announcement "Be not afraid!" Since talking was difficult for me, people texted and emailed: my sister several times a day, members of my religious community, friends, and parishioners, all texting their love and prayers for me. Facebook friends prayed online for me. When I could not pray for myself, all these people prayed for me. Their prayers breathed for me. They still do.

Gradually, the virus lessened its hold on me. It was not going to clog my lungs. It would let me sleep. It would let me be aware and, for increasing moments, alert. I was weakened but going to survive. From the news, I learned the virus created a worldwide community of the suffering, with me among the most fortunate. I would hear a consistent wail of ambulance sirens carrying those sicker than I to an emergency room. They were part of me, so wordlessly, automatically, I prayed for us. The Latin chant for Easter, the *Regina Coeli*, came unbidden into my mind, and, with inner music I had not summoned, I entrusted the sick—including me—to whatever God would do with us.

My first intentional prayer was watching Pope Francis pray in a desolate and deserted St. Peter's Square. I don't remember anything he said, nor the words to any of the prayers, but I do remember the stark picture of him: sitting in the rain, praying, for all those around the world, the dead, the grieving, the medical personnel, the recovering, for me. As I watched him sit there, an early childhood memory materialized. I remembered my father, on Holy Thursday, taking me by the hand for Holy Thursday services at our parish of Holy Redeemer. The ceremonies were extravagant, with choirs, processions, stripping the altar, the tabernacle gaping open with the reservation of the blessed sacrament in an elaborate altar of reservation. Neighborhood children plundered flowers from gardens to adorn the shrine. I did not know why we were kneeling before the side altar. "This is Jesus in jail after he was arrested, and we must keep him company" is how my father explained it to me. We walked to churches in neighborhoods I was forbidden to cross the street to visit: St. Michaels, St. Theresa, St. Josaphat, St. Mark, St. Henry, St. Stanislaus. We visited Jesus in his side altar jail in each church, saying a prayer, keeping him company. In St. Peter's Basilica, Pope Francis was sitting before the blessed sacrament, keeping all those imprisoned by COVID-19 company. I sat with him, Pope Francis in the rain, me in my armchair, joining his prayer for so many.

That night, and the next morning, and every day after that, I would pray for the ill, those who cared for them, for the dead and their loved ones, for all those out of work—worried, anxious about housing, food, the future. A question haunted me, and haunts me still: Why me?

Why am I recovering while so many are not? What does it mean? Do not misunderstand me, I do not believe God kills some people and saves favorites. We are loved equally in the eyes of the God who made us out of love, for love; made, Jesus tells us, for life to the full. Perhaps there is no reason why I contracted a less virulent strain of the virus while more saintly and self-sacrificing souls contracted the more lethal version. I felt fear for the first time, fear of the fragility of life that spares some and strikes others down. This fear taught me that while I do not know why I am alive and others not, it is the responsibility of the living to pray for those who died and those they left behind.

Within a few days, it would be Palm Sunday and then Holy Week, a Holy Week unlike any other, a Holy Week so dangerous people could not go to a church to pray. Quarantined, I could not go to a church. I did what I have never done in my forty-one years of priesthood: celebrated a private Mass. A brother priest left a Mass kit outside my door, and, on Palm Sunday, I celebrated a Eucharist I will not soon forget. I was overwhelmed with a profound feeling of gratitude for the gift of my life, not simply that I survived but that I was alive at all! Thanksgiving poured through the readings, the passion, the words of the liturgy. The Mass went slowly, offered with deep gratitude for those whose prayers and love breathed for me, gratitude for those protecting and nursing my quarantine; with prayer for those suffering alone, dying alone, and for those who could not see their dying loved ones, could not bury them nor hold each other in grief. Receiving the Eucharist, in communion with the risen Lord, I was in communion with all those the Crucified One loves and holds dear. The final blessing was God's blessing upon the city outside my bedroom window. I am a preacher. Capturing what I could of the Holy Spirit's whispers during that Eucharist, I posted my digital homily to my quarantined city:

It happened so fast.
So very fast.
Sunday was well, happy, triumphant.
Thursday night, we gathered for Passover.
The next night, he was dead, buried by
    strangers.
Over and done in five short days.
It never struck me before—reading
    St. Matthew's passion
—as it strikes me now.
But now everything happens so fast.
People are sick and die, in less time.
The matriarch of a large Toms River Italian
    family
Dying without knowing two sons died before
    her.
Within the week, a New York physician dying
    in his husband's arms,
Nurses across the street making gowns of
    hefty bags,
Respiratory therapists asleep on their feet.
Everyone out of work—no rent, no food, no
    hugs, no future.
I went to work one Monday,
Was sick by nightfall, and next I knew—or
    didn't know
—it was Sunday: which one?
It all happened within a week, to all of us...
Milan, China, Spain, New York, everywhere.

No time to prepare, to react, to grieve, to
    think of any future.
The world ends quickly—even for Jesus.
This Sunday we wave no comforting palms.
Comfort is found knowing the speed of
    disaster,
The speed of our surprise, suffering, grief,
Is shared by the swiftly Crucified
Who with dizzying speed raises us, as he was
    raised
—into life with time only for love.
Amen.[3]

The virus left behind a mere shell of vitality, which took longer to replenish than I anticipated. Recovery time was filled with anxiety by the world news penetrating my quarantine. The numbers of those who died in New York rapidly increased, day after day after day. Working from home and social distancing were luxuries many could not afford, and the most vulnerable were disproportionately represented among the dead. Nursing homes could not protect their sick and elderly, and they too joined the torrential numbers of the dead. What was hidden in Wuhan was now manifest, as the wingspan of this disease covered Europe, Great Britain, Ireland, Canada, and reached across to India and Pakistan. Infected, the world's economy was collapsing, and hunger was growing exponentially in Africa, South America, India, the Philippines. In the United States, unemployment reached proportions not seen since the Great Depression in the 1930s. Helpless...I felt helpless not just about my body, but my country and my world.

At the time of this writing, the virus is not under control. While diminishing in some locations, in others it flares into "hot spots." In my country, testing is evasive and vaccination is an unrealized hope for perhaps years to come. It is apparent that we are not going to reopen as much as we must reinvent ourselves, beginning again, with the parameters of our new life dictated by an enemy we have not conquered and whose reinvasion we fear.

Churches are closed. People cannot visit us; we cannot visit them. Digital efforts to broadcast the Mass and preach the gospel have intensified but are reaching only a fraction of our people. How can you be Catholic without community, without Eucharist? Yet, to do what we do best is infectious, a danger to the people of God. I am a priest ordained to Word, Sacrament, and Service, and the structures of that ministry are unavailable and their future unknown. Helplessness becomes frustration and frustration becomes anger. The longer the pandemic continues, the more likely anger will accompany it, one more deadly by-product of COVID-19.

Frustration, grief, and anger blind us. Enveloped in their haze, we are unable to recognize the risen Lord. Easter is hard to believe much less celebrate. I realized, through these words of Cardinal Carlo Martini, that I had been looking for Easter in all the wrong places:

> God did not perform any miracles to save Jesus from death, God is always with Jesus, on his side, and validating him. Therefore, it is not through amazingly powerful miracles, but in being with each one of us in our trials, in keeping company even in the deep recesses of our loneliness, in being close to our distress with the hope of eternal life, that God reveals to be the "God with us," the God and Father of

our Lord Jesus. God is everywhere someone suffers like Jesus, wherever someone dies like Jesus, wherever someone lives and suffers for love, for truth, for justice, for the poor; God is there to lessen the suffering of the world: This is the God of Jesus who is proclaimed in Jesus' resurrection.[4]

The virus has closed the structures of the Church but has not drained the life of the Church that is the people of God. Every night, at 7 o'clock, people around the world come to their balconies, open their windows, or come to their front door to applaud the sacrificial love of everyone who works in health care: doctors, nurses, respiratory therapists, orderlies, sanitation workers, ambulance drivers; their love and sacrifice is obvious. The Spirit of the risen Lord breathes through them.

The Spirit breathes through actions of kindness and mercy that have arisen with this pandemic. I think of the almost daily news stories of people who deliver groceries to neighbors. Owners of shuttered restaurants now cook for those who can no longer afford to buy their own groceries. People spend their quarantine sewing essential face masks for those without. Business owners reconfigured their workshops to make needed hospital gowns, converted factories to make ventilators.

Ordinary actions are now heroic, with bus and subway drivers, grocery store clerks, truck drivers, police, and firefighters daily risking contact with this contagious virus so everyone else can go to work, buy groceries, remain protected. Teachers must now prepare new online lessons for students who cannot leave home. Parents quarantined with their children, spouses with one another, and roommates, unable to get away from each other, demonstrate added patience, kindness, a willingness to forgive and give of themselves. Friends make special efforts to reach out to friends they cannot visit. In a grim fashion, the funeral directors are now charged with the corporal work of mercy to bury the dead loved ones cannot. Pope Francis calls these actions "everyday holiness." They are everyday manifestations of the risen Lord. People may not be able to go to church, synagogue, or mosque, but that has not prevented them from breathing holiness into a world chocked with virus.

My story of COVID-19 concludes with a lesson: a virus invisible to the eye is teaching the world just how fragile and interconnected we truly are. This interconnection is not simply an occasion for sickness, it is an opportunity for communion. In the end, we are connected to God only by love. The risen Lord Jesus remains connected to us by love, a love that connects us to each other through lives of service, mercy, and kindness. This is how we will defeat the virus and rebuild our world.

Notes

1. I am a member of the Missionary Society of St. Paul, known as the Paulist Fathers, the first religious order of men founded in the United States.

2. Oblate Sisters of Jesus the Priest, dedicated to praying for and ministering to seminarians and priests.

3. Mark David Janus, CSP, PhD, Palm Sunday 2020.

4. Carlo Martini, *Disciples of the Risen Christ: Carlo Martini on Lent and Easter* (Mahwah, NJ: Paulist Press, 2016).